Romans

by Robert Jewett

General Editor, Lynne M. Deming
Assistant Editor, Margaret Rogers
Copy Processing, Sylvia Marlow
Cover Design by Harriet Bateman

ISBN 0-939-697-30-0

Table of Contents

Outline of Romans

Introduction to Romans

Paul's letter to the Romans was probably written from Corinth in the winter of A.D. 56-57. In the letter itself, Paul mentions his host, Gaius of Corinth (16:23), and recommends Phoebe, from the nearby town of Cenchreae (16:1). Thus we may conclude that the letter was written during the three-month period that Paul spent in or around Corinth (see the note in Acts 20:3). This period was just prior to Paul's departure to deliver the Jerusalem offering.

The Form of the Original Letter

Although there are many textual variants related to the final chapters of Romans, it now appears certain that Paul's original letter contained sixteen chapters. The only portions that may not stem from Paul are the closing benediction (16:25-27) and the warning against heretics that breaks up the sequence of greetings (16:17-20). Thus it is essential to take the material from the final chapters into account in considering the purpose and character of Romans.

The Nature and Purpose of Romans

Paul dictated this letter to solicit help from the Roman house churches in the planning and logistical support for a mission to Spain (see 15:24, 28). The theological argument is designed to unify the competitive house churches in Rome so they will be willing and able to cooperate in this effort. The power of the gospel (1:16) to achieve the unification of all nations (15:7-13) provides the imperative for this mission and therefore stands at the heart of Romans.

Romans 1:1-15

Introduction to These Verses

Romans is the only Pauline letter addressed to a church
that he did not found. This means that Paul has to
introduce himself in a way that is very different from his
other letters. The first fifteen verses of Chapter 1 provide
this self-introduction. Paul needs to explain why he is
writing and identify who he is. As we know from general
experience, first impressions mean a lot. So the way Paul
introduces himself and approaches the congregation at
Rome will have a great deal to do with how he will be
received.

The Situation in Rome

Although Paul has never been to Rome, he clearly has
a firm grasp of the situation there. He mentions in
Romans 1:8 that their faith was proclaimed *in all the
world*. He also mentions in 1:13 that he had *often intended
to come to you*, which indicates that he had studied and
thought about the Roman church situation for a long
time. We know that he was a missionary partner for a
number of years with Roman refugees, Prisca (Priscilla)
and Aquila, mentioned in Acts 18:1-3 and 18:26. That
Prisca and Aquila are now back in Rome at the time of
writing is indicated by Romans 16:3-5. So we have every
reason to believe that Paul had heard frequent reports
about the situation in Rome.

It appears that the Roman churches were founded

sometime in the decade of the thirties or early forties by anonymous Christian missionaries traveling to Rome. The most likely centers for the earliest congregations were the small Greek-speaking Jewish synagogues whose presence in Rome has been proven by archaeology and other historical research. These synagogues were quite small and local in their background. The synagogues attracted people who had immigrated to Rome from a particular part of the Roman empire. Most of the inscriptions found in these synagogues are in Greek, which indicates that the language used by the Jewish community in Rome was primarily Greek, rather than Latin or Hebrew. Another peculiarity was the lack of a centralized organization for the synagogues. This had a serious consequence for the development both of Judaism and Christianity in Rome.

When conflicts began to emerge between Christian missionaries and their zealous Jewish opponents in the late forties, the Roman authorities had no organization to consult. Concerned about public disorder, the government simply closed all the synagogues and expelled the agitators. This event, the so-called "Edict of Claudius," probably occurred in A.D. 49, which correlates closely with Prisca's and Aquila's arrival in Corinth as refugees when they first met Paul. The result was that the early Christian communities were now forced to discover new leaders and new locations for their common life. The impression of recent scholars is that the Christian groups formed themselves into house churches, at least five in number, with new leaders who had not been affected by the expulsion of the Jewish Christian missionaries.

In the years between 49 and 54 it appears that the Roman house churches developed in distinctive and independent ways, in some instances departing quite drastically from their roots in the synagogues where they had been founded. Charismatic leaders came to the fore in some of these churches and, in several instances at least, well-to-do patrons and patronesses who had means to provide a house became prominent leaders. It was probably during this period that some anti-Semitic tendencies visible in Romans 9–11 began to become prominent. Feelings of superiority on the part of Gentile Christian house churches in relation to Jewish Christian groups began to emerge.

After the death of the emperor Claudius in 54 it appears that the Jewish Christians were allowed to return to Rome and the synagogues were allowed to reopen. It was during this period that conflicts began to arise that are dealt with in the latter chapters of Romans. When the Jewish Christian leaders like Prisca and Aquila began to return they found that the churches in which they earlier had been members were drastically altered because of new leaders and the new settings of house churches. In all probability the conservative order of worship based on the Jewish prayer book was no longer in effect. New charismatic forms of worship and new hymns that came from different branches of early Christianity were being used. Conflicts over leadership began to surface when the Gentile Christian leaders of house churches resisted the resumption of leadership roles by Jewish Christian missionaries who were returning. Conflicts involved conservative versus liberal theology, charismatic versus traditional orders of service, Jewish versus Gentile patterns of ethics, different church calendars, and a variety of other issues, not all of which are reflected in Romans itself.

In this situation, the terms "weak" and "strong" were used, probably to indicate the outlook of groups that we would today identify roughly as conservative or liberal. The term "strong" was evidently used by the majority of Gentile Christians who felt strong enough to break free from the Jewish law and calendar. They used the derogatory term "weak" to designate the conservatives who did not feel free to break from the traditional patterns of worship and belief that they had inherited from their Jewish tradition. But the way these terms are used in Romans 14–15 indicates that the conflicts were not simply between Jewish Christian conservatives and Gentile liberal Christians. There is evidence that there were both conservative and liberal Jewish Christians and conservative and liberal Gentile Christians. The situation was quite tangled and the conflicts at the time that Paul wrote the letter, in the winter of A.D. 56-57, appear to have been quite intense.

The Address of Romans

The situation of church conflict helps to explain the level of tact with which Paul addresses the Roman house churches and also the peculiar address of the letter. In Romans 1:6-7 Paul addresses the Christians *in Rome*, but does not refer to them as a church. These verses contain three fairly distinct identifications of the Christians, which probably reflects Paul's knowledge of how the Christians identified themselves. It is likely that the liberals, or the "strong," identified themselves as "the called of Jesus Christ," stressing their election and thus their superior status. The conservatives, or the "weak," probably identified themselves as the the ones "called to be saints." This would indicate the high priority given to moral standards, in some instances based on the Old Testament law.

The middle address in the beginning of verse 7 is probably Paul's effort to find a unification formula: *to all God's beloved in Rome*. Paul's effort is to find an inclusive basis for the church, a motivation for mutual acceptance. He stresses at this point and throughout the letter that each Christian is unconditionally loved by God, that both conservatives and liberals are recipients of God's grace. In this and in many other ways Paul seeks to find a common ground that will unite the competing house churches and the various leaders now present in Rome. This effort at unification is one of the keys to understanding the first fifteen verses and, indeed, the whole letter.

Paul's Goal in Writing

The introduction of a Pauline letter is a primary place to discover the purpose of writing. While many elaborate theories have been constructed to explain Paul's purpose, it is best to take into account what Paul actually says in these opening verses. In Romans 1:11 he says he wants to see the Romans in order to impart a *spiritual gift to strengthen* them. This is further explained in 1:15 as preaching *the gospel*.

Clearly, however, Paul does not wish to give the impression that the Roman house churches lack a legitimate gospel. He says in verse 12 that he wishes to be *mutually encouraged by each other's faith, both yours and mine*. That he does not consider their faith deficient is also indicated by verse 8, in which he expresses gratitude that *your faith is proclaimed in all the world*. Why, then, does Paul wish to preach in Rome? The puzzle is deepened by the fact that Paul mentions his standard missionary procedure in Romans 15:20, not to preach in an area where someone else has witnessed, *lest I build on another man's foundation*.

There are several clues in this introduction to solve this puzzle. Paul places both his work and the faith of the Roman house churches in a global context. He refers in verse 5 to his apostolic task to *bring about the obedience of faith* in all nations. There is another expression of this theme in verse 13 in which the work in Rome is set in the context of *the rest of the Gentiles*. In the following verse he states the worldwide horizon of his missionary obligation.

Therefore, we can be certain that Paul's preaching in Rome is directly related to world mission. When Paul returns to this theme in 15:24 we discover what this means. He discloses his plan to establish a Christian mission in Spain, which was then perceived to be the end of the civilized world. Paul hopes to involve the Romans in the planning and support of this mission. This means that Paul's letter to the Romans needs to be understood as a missionary letter. It sets forth the gospel that Paul wishes to preach but also aims at finding common ground between the splintered factions of the Roman house churches so that they will stop fighting with one another and cooperate in this common mission. Church politics and world mission are here closely united.

This section of Romans has two main parts.

I. The Beginning of Paul's Letter (1:1-7)
II. The Announcement of Paul's Mission (1:8-15)

The Beginning of Paul's Letter (1:1–7)

The opening verse has a word that is often rendered differently in modern translations. The literal translation is *slave*, though it is often downplayed with the translation *servant*. The translation *slave* is often felt to be far too humble for the high apostolic office that Paul claims in verses 1-5.

Actually the term *slave* had a formal bureaucratic connotation for the Roman audience. The Roman bureaucracy, which was rapidly developing at the time Paul wrote this letter, consisted of highly-trained and highly-paid slaves of Caesar. These persons were preferred in the imperial offices because they were loyal to the emperor alone, hoping for their freedom after some years of loyal service. Many of these slaves serving in the imperial bureaucracy became fabulously rich because of their handling of imperial finances. Also during the time Paul wrote, the expression "slave of Caesar" was used for imperial ambassadors or representatives of various kinds. It was felt that such persons carried the majesty and power of the emperor as they represented him in foreign courts.

The opening words of Romans could therefore be

translated, *Paul, an ambassador of Jesus Christ*. The idea here is consistent with the expression "apostle," which meant a messenger or a person sent for a specific message and mission. The term was often used in secular settings for a representative sent off on an errand by someone else. In this instance Paul qualifies the term *apostle* by the expression *called*, referring to his election to missionary activity at the time of his conversion.

The early Christian creed cited in 1:3-4 begins after the word *Son*. A literal translation is as follows: *born from David's seed according to the flesh, appointed Son of God in power according to the spirit of holiness, through the resurrection of the dead*.

There is evidence that this confession originated in Jewish Christian circles with a stress on the messianic line from David and the appointment as Son of God through the Resurrection. This early creed is very close to some of the creeds found in the Book of Acts, stressing the seed of David and the adoption of Jesus as the Son of God on the basis of the Resurrection.

This early creed was apparently edited by liberal hellenistic Christians who wished to downplay the nationalistic component of David's seed and to stress the power of the Spirit. They inserted the lines *according to the flesh* and *according to the Spirit* in order to affirm that the business of David's seed was only on a fleshly and therefore human level, whereas the appointment of Jesus as the Son of God was by direct divine intervention, according to the Spirit. This edition tended to universalize the creed, opening it up to people who were not of Jewish background and who were not loyal to the messianic hope of Israel.

It appears that the final change made to the creed was effected by Paul himself, adding the words *of holiness* to the phrase *according to the Spirit*. This additional phrase counters the tendency of those persons in the early church who liked to think in dualistic terms, opposing flesh to Spirit. As we know from the Corinthian letters in particular, the liberals who were most conscious of being in the Spirit tended at times to believe that they were superior to "fleshly" rules such as the Ten Commandments.

The problem of libertinism, of believing that one is above the law, is countered at a number of other points in the argument of Romans, which indicates that this was something of a problem in the Roman house churches. By emphasizing holiness Paul makes clear that the spirit of a new age is consistent with ethical responsibility. This is also an important motif in Wesleyan theology because Wesley's idea of "scriptural holiness" comes in part from Romans. Paul shared Wesley's emphasis that the new birth should result in new behavior which is ethically responsible.

In 1:5 Paul shifts from the first person singular to the first person plural: *We have received grace and apostleship.* Paul often speaks of himself in the first person plural and in many instances he is referring to himself and his coworkers. Paul had a shared sense of missionary obligation. Most of his letters are written by himself in collaboration with his missionary colleagues. Since the Romans did not know Paul and his missionary team, it was inappropriate in this instance to mention them in the opening chapter. But it is worth observing that in Chapter 16 Paul mentions greetings from Timothy and a number of other close colleagues.

Unlike the other letters addressed to various Pauline congregations, there is no reference in 1:7 to the church in Rome. This is perhaps due to the fact that only one of the five house churches mentioned in Chapter 15 referred to itself as a church. Keep in mind that Romans was written at a time before there was a standard set of terms used for early Christians. Each congregation probably called itself something different, particularly in a place where the church was as decentralized as it was in Rome.

The Announcement of Paul's Mission (1:8-15)

The stress on inclusiveness is carried on in verse 8, where Paul in the thanksgiving refers to *all of you* as the subject of his prayers. Sensitivity to congregational feelings is also manifest in verses 11 and 12. In verse 11 Paul boldly states that he wishes to impart a *spiritual charisma* or blessing, which might have been taken to imply that Paul did not feel that the congregation had spiritual power and fell short in some way.

Paul immediately adds the tactful words in verse 12 to make clear that he expects to learn as much as he teaches when he comes to Rome.

In verse 13, where Paul provides the narration of events behind his planned visit, there is a reference to the hindrances that have prevented his earlier arrival. See 2 Corinthians 11:24-28 for an example of the kind of hindrances Paul had in mind.

By correlating the details of 2 Corinthians 8 and 9 with the indications of the problem in collecting the Jerusalem offering, it is clear that the discord in Corinth set Paul's plan back for at least a year. Also there were several imprisonments during this time. Acts 20:1-3 indicates other reasons for delays, namely, the hostility of Jewish zealots against Paul that was behind some of Paul's other imprisonments and troubles as well. His hope, as evident in Romans 15, had been to complete his work in the eastern mission field, deliver the offering, and arrive in Rome in order to get to Spain as quickly as possible. His plans were delayed several years by the adversity that Paul had experienced.

In 1:14 Paul describes his sense of obligation in language that may seem somewhat repulsive. In the Greco-Roman world the term *barbarian* indicated someone who could not speak Latin or Greek. The negative connotation was related both to language ability and cultural awkwardness. The term *barbarian* would have included many Jews as well as the great bulk of the population in Spain.

The second set of categories, *the wise* and *the foolish*, probably relates to educational level. We might think of the wise as the highly educated and the foolish as working class people and slaves who did not have the benefit of higher education. It is important to observe that Paul stresses his obligation to both of these stereotypes. It is therefore clear that in the church, stereotypes like this are under attack. The implication of verse 15 is that all of these groups are represented in Rome and that Paul's broad sense of responsibility leads him to include everyone.

§ § § § § § §

The Message of Romans 1:1-15

Paul's approach is an intriguing model for the way we should interact with each other in the church. Although he is obviously quite concerned about some of the tensions within the congregation and provides a very elaborate theological rationale for how the gospel should be understood, he nevertheless respects their achievements and their viewpoint. Such tact is directly related to the gospel as Paul sets it forth in Romans.

The essence of the gospel relates to the grace of God shown in Jesus Christ. When people internalize God's love they are capable of accepting one another and respecting one another more fully. Rather than seeking to impose their views on others, they learn to respect people with whom they disagree. This kind of tact is as crucial for the life of modern congregations as it was in Paul's time.

The opening verses of Romans call us to reflect on the relationship between diversity and inclusiveness. Paul mentions in verse 3 that he has been prevented from visiting Rome repeatedly in the past. Both he and the Romans had faced adversity. When we think back on the life of our churches over the past few years, we can remember similar conflicts and adverse circumstances that we have had to surmount. The frequent and often unwilling movement of our people from one community to another produces the kind of pain that the Roman refugees had experienced. Then, as now, such adversity caused groups to become hostile to one another.

From the opening lines of Romans, Paul makes a case for an inclusive gospel. He seeks to include all those in Rome and believes that his gospel is relevant for all the nations. He explicitly includes the people of different educational levels and different language backgrounds in his identification of the gospel.

As the argument of Romans will make plain in subsequent chapters, Paul's conviction is that the grace of God holds persons in adversity firmly in the hollow of God's hand. Nothing can separate us from the love of Christ. The gospel of Christ reveals that God's love stands behind us even in the worst of circumstances. This is why Paul speaks of himself as *under obligation* (Romans 1:14) because the gospel compels him to seek the unity of the church and the unification of the human race. The gospel sets no boundaries, then or now. This is a splendid resource to help us cope with the conflicts between groups and individuals today.

§ § § § § § §

Romans 1:16-32

Introduction to These Verses

With Romans 1:16 Paul opens up the formal argument
of his letter. It is very important to keep the purpose of
this abstract argument in mind. It clarifies the gospel that
he intends to proclaim in Spain. It also has a particular
bearing on the Roman house churches, as seen in the
emphasis on inclusiveness between Jews and Gentiles.
Paul sees in the gospel the basis for unifying the church.
This interest is also visible in the opening section of his
argument dealing with human idolatry and divine wrath
(1:18-32).

While it may strike modern readers as puzzling that
Paul would begin on such a negative note, his purpose is
to shatter the pretensions dividing the Roman house
churches. Before he can make a case that the Christians
in Rome are equal in grace he must first prove that they
are equal under wrath. Only when the claims of
superiority by the "weak" and the "strong" are destroyed
will the Christians in Rome really be in a position to
understand fully how the righteous must live by faith
alone (1:17). These verses may be divided into two parts.

I. The Gospel as Divine Power (1:16-17)
II. Human Idolatry and Divine Wrath (1:18-32)

The Gospel as Divine Power (1:16-17)

The formal argument of Romans opens with a thesis
statement in 1:16-17. The major themes in the first four

chapters are stated here. Paul begins as an ambassador would—with the themes of shame and power. An ambassador lacks credibility if the power he represents is weak. Paul therefore opens with the bold assurance, *I am not ashamed of the gospel*. The power that Paul represents is superior to that of Rome itself. Paul is convinced that the gospel of the death and resurrection of Jesus Christ has the capacity to conquer the world. Therefore, the stress that the gospel places on the power of God is one of the most remarkable features of Romans.

Paul contends that the gospel has the power for salvation for everyone who has faith. The scope of this power is truly universal, promising nothing less than the salvation of the entire human race.

In 1:17 Paul explains the content of the gospel and connects it with the *righteousness of God*. When this expression is linked with the phrase *is revealed*, we are brought into the context of the Jewish expectation that at the end of time God would be revealed, would triumph over enemies, and would bring the kingdom of God to the earth. Righteousness in this context is closely related to glory. When God's glory is manifest, righteousness is achieved and the world is restored to its original intent.

This idea of the restoration of the righteousness of God through the creation of righteousness for persons is related naturally to the Creation story in Jewish theology. In Genesis 2 and 3 the first humans chose to disobey God and sought to take over the position of God. They fell prey to the temptation to be *like God, knowing good and evil* (Genesis 3:5). This caused the corruption of the human race and of the earth itself, for the curse that followed the fall of humankind involved the soil that resisted human effort and caused the anguish of human labor.

The conception in popular theology of the first century was that the righteousness of God had departed from the earth as well as from humans. So when Paul expresses the conviction that in the gospel *the righteousness of God is revealed,* he is contending that humans as well as the ecology of their planet are to be restored to reflect the righteousness of God.

In contrast to the popular view, salvation is not simply the "justification" of individuals. It is a social and individual transformation that occurs from faith to faith. The faith of persons who have responded to the gospel is caught by others because the gospel itself has the power to evoke faith. Faith in this context is not so much belief as it is a faithful response. The salvation of the world consists of persons not only receiving the gospel but also living it, setting the whole creation right.

The citation from Habakkuk 2:4 that Paul uses at the end of verse 17 is slightly altered to fit into the context. In a way that is unparalleled in the Hebrew tradition, Paul emphasizes in his use of this sentence that a response to the gospel in faith is the key to genuine life. Having faith in this context is clearly understood as faith in the gospel. It means forming one's life and allowing one's actions to be shaped by the righteousness of God as revealed in the Christ event.

The Hebrew tradition, on the other hand, stresses that those who are faithful to the law shall be preserved by God's righteousness. There is a dramatic shift in the direction of conversion through the preaching of the gospel in the Christian use of this line from Habakkuk. There is also a significant emphasis on universality in the words, *to every one who has faith, to the Jew first and also to the Greek.* Jewish priority in the chronological sense is preserved because it was from the Jewish people that the gospel emerged and that the Christ came. But as far as righteousness is concerned, Paul argues that everyone stands on an equal basis.

The Issue of Defining Righteousness

The peculiarity of the English language and the tradition of translating Romans leads to some difficulties in understanding the term *righteousness*. English provides two different words for what in the original text of Romans was a single family of terms. We speak of *righteousness* and *justification*, both of which have rather different connotations in English.

The difficulty is particularly visible in the thesis of Romans 1:17. Often this verse is translated in the direction of the *righteousness of God* being revealed in the gospel, with the following citation translated as *the just shall live by faith*. The problem is that the word *just* comes from exactly the same stem as the term *righteousness*. When this translation problem is not understood, as is so frequently the case in the Protestant tradition, *justification by faith alone* gets entirely separated from the *righteousness of God*. That is, God's activity in transforming humans is understood as the gift of forgiveness which allows us to be justified, even though we have violated the law. However, we must understand that in Pauline theology, being justified is very different from being righteous. In fact, Paul wishes to speak of humans in this entire letter as being "rightwised," a term from old English that would be better used in place of *justify* in the translation for Romans. To rightwise is to make right, to set one right, and to achieve a transformation in which humans come to reflect the righteousness of God.

The difficulty is to connect righteousness with a traditional understanding of justification. An old-fashioned view, frequently found in some of the older commentaries, is that righteousness is the standard for what is right for God as well as for humans. When this rather moralistic interpretation of righteousness becomes central, it leads inevitably to a moralistic understanding of what human salvation means. It can end up in a new form of the law, a major problem for Romans. That is, people can be led to think that if they simply conform to the high standards of the Christian faith they are justified.

Another approach was shaped by Luther in particular. In this tradition, justification or rightwising is understood to be the gift of freedom from condemnation. The difficulty with this interpretation, whether in its moralistic or abstract theological form, is that the parallel Paul wishes to create in Romans 1:17 between the righteousness of God and the rightwising of humans is lost.

The viewpoint advocated in this commentary is that the righteousness of God in Romans refers to God's capacity to impose righteousness on the world. God has a claim on the creation that it reflect divine righteousness. When Paul speaks of the righteousness of God as being revealed, he is operating out of the Jewish tradition of God standing triumphant at the end of history after vanquishing or transforming all foes.

This interpretation allows us to see the close parallel between the righteousness of God and the righteousness given to humans. When humans are caught up in the divine plan and made to conform to the divine will, they enter into a relationship with God that has righteousness as its major component. They achieve the goal for which they were created.

A proper understanding of righteousness implies that salvation must be understood in a collective sense. When communities are captured by the righteousness of God they become agents of the divine will over the whole created order. Paul offers a concept of the gospel that trusts the will of God to regain control over the whole creation. This view provides a basis for a world mission that transforms individuals as well as the principalities and powers, regaining and restoring the corrupted world itself.

In this sense, when Paul refers to *the righteousness of God*, he is very close to the Old Testament idea that the glory of God is manifest when God wins a victory over enemies.

Human Idolatry and Divine Wrath (1:18-32)

The formal argument of Romans begins with 1:18. Like other Hebrew thinkers, Paul conceives of wrath as an expression of righteousness. God will prevail even against opposition. But unlike most discussions of wrath, Paul begins with an intrinsic doctrine of wrath. He suggests that wrath begins as the natural consequence of breaking the moral law. An inevitable law of cause and effect goes into effect whenever humans set themselves up in opposition to God.

Romans 1:18 contends that the core of the human dilemma is suppression of the truth. This radical doctrine of sin, which presupposes that all humans have within themselves an innate tendency to resist God, is a radicalization of the story of the fall of the human race as seen in light of the Christ event. When humans encountered the pure goodness of Jesus, their impulse was to snuff him out. This desire to suppress the truth is understood in Romans as the essence of human sin.

To make this case, Paul suggests in 1:19 and 20 that truth has always been available to humans. God's nature is manifest in the created order. Humans are capable of grasping the difference between themselves and God by looking at the grandeur and intricacy of the world about them. They can dimly grasp God's power, but the tendency of humans interpreted in the light of the Christ event again is to suppress this knowledge. Rather than acknowledging our limitations, our human tendency is to try to make ourselves more than we are. We respond to the feelings of vulnerability that we have by claiming to be invulnerable. We wish to suppress the fact that we as creatures are different from the Creator.

In the language of 1:21, humans glorify themselves rather than God. We seek to place ourselves at the center of the universe. We fall into pride. The language that Paul uses to describe this is quite general. It would be understood equally by persons coming from the Greek and Roman philosophical tradition and from persons coming from the Hebrew background.

Paul's desire is to make a universal case about the nature of human sin. But it is a case directly shaped by the revelation of the gospel. Only in the cross of Christ is this deep human hostility against God truly visible; only there is the human suppression manifest in its ultimate form. And if we are honest with ourselves, we each realize that we would do the very same thing. We too would have cried "Crucify him!" or at least would have fled and left him in the lurch. The universal human betrayal, deriving from our desire to preserve ourselves and to be invulnerable, is manifest in the cross event.

Paul goes on to argue in 1:21-22 that there are three immediate consequences of suppressing the truth. When persons begin to confuse themselves with God, their mental capacity is fatally crippled. They begin to lie about themselves and about the realities around them. Refusing to recognize the truth about themselves, and constantly trying to rearrange the facts to make them look better, their very minds become *darkened*. Paul uses the word *heart* at this point, designating that the very center of human compassion and judgment is eroded.

We know this process from recent political experience. When people begin to cover up the truth, their human sympathy becomes eroded as well. They begin to treat persons as things, to misuse them in order to protect their own reputations or otherwise to achieve their own purposes. Finally, in their effort to prove themselves wise, they become fools. The mark of a fool is the lack of knowledge and recognition of limitations. If the essence of sin is the failure to recognize human limitations, the confusion between ourselves and God, then folly is the logical consequence.

Paul illustrates this foolishness in verse 23 with what were perceived as the silliest forms of idolatry: worshiping *birds and animals and serpents*. When God is no longer worshiped, mortal objects are. Today we might replace the bird with a dollar bill, the serpent with a flag, or an ordinary person with one of the current superstars. But the reality would be precisely the same. Glorifying the creature rather than the Creator is always the final sign of human stupidity.

In verses 24-31 Paul describes the social consequences of the failure to recognize the difference between the creature and the Creator. Three times Paul repeats the line that *God gave them up* to the consequences of their deeds. The perversion having started with the darkening of the human mind and the twisting of moral sensitivity, the punishment is to live in the midst of that twistedness. Paul asserts that God enters into the process of the moral law, confirming the judgment against humans in the form of wrath. In one sense it is a self-imposed wrath, originated by humans turning away from the truth toward falsehood. But in another sense, it is a wrath that God supports and sustains. It consists not in fiery punishments at the end of time, but rather in the perversion and twistedness of human relationships in the here and now.

Paul places in this context the twistedness of sexual relations (verses 26-27). In contrast to some moralists who believe that Paul is creating here a law concerning homosexuality, it is clear that he views the twistedness as itself a sign and punishment of divine wrath. The evil quality of such perversion is simply assumed by Paul, in accordance with the shared legacy of Judaism and early Christianity.

The twenty-one forms of evil that Paul lists in 1:29-31 are likewise not the cause of divine wrath, but its expression. When one reads through this list it is as if the lid of chaos has been opened up, Pandora's box broken wide, with human evil tumbling out in its manifold forms, swarming over society and destroying every good hope. We can look about us in our society, and at times we can even look within ourselves, and see the evidence of this flood of chaotic evil. But its cause is the refusal to recognize the Creator, as verse 25 makes plain. The essence of the human problem derives from exchanging *the truth about God for a lie and worshiped and served the creature rather than the Creator*. Thus in verse 25 Paul returns to his basic thesis that sin is the suppression of truth about ourselves, the confusion of ourselves with God. Wrath is the inevitable consequence.

§ § § § § § §

The Message of Romans 1:16-32

Nowhere else in the Greco-Roman world or in ancient
Judaism does one have so strong an emphasis on the
conscious repudiation of the knowledge of God on the
part of humankind. Paul's emphasis on suppressing the
truth about God as the essence of sin, and his contention
that humans tend to confuse themselves with the divine,
set him off from his contemporaries in the ancient world.
The radical side of his idea of a natural revelation
consciously perverted by humans can best be explained
on the basis of Paul's theology of the cross.

Paul discovered in the Christ event the depth of human
perversion and twistedness, and the tendency of humans
to reject the truth and to deny its validity for their lives,
even to the point of killing the Christ when they had him
in their grasp. This idea of a radical and universal fall of
humans is what gives Paul's argument its particular
sharpness and its relevance for the modern world as well.

§ § § § § § §

Romans 2

Introduction to This Chapter

With Romans 2:1-16, we encounter some of the most difficult and hotly disputed lines in Paul's letter to the Romans. Here he deals with issues that are directly relevant to the Roman house churches. The repeated references to judging in verses 1-3 are strongly reminiscent of the tendency that Paul sees in the Roman congregation, which was split between the weak and the strong (Romans 14). It is well, therefore, to bring the material of Romans 14:4 and 10 into Paul's argument here. Paul suggests that when humans judge one another they lose sight of the distinction between the creature and the Creator. Also, the reference to despising God's kindness in verse 4 seems to relate quite closely to the material in Romans 14:10: *Why do you despise your brother?*

Here is an outline of this chapter.

I. The Judgmental Spirit (2:1-5)
II. Judgment According to Works (2:6-7)
III. The Relevance of Impartiality (2:8-16)
IV. No Exemption by Religious Status (2:17-29)
    A. Claims of religious superiority (2:17-20)
    B. Rhetorical questions (2:21-23)
    C. No exemption through circumcision (2:25-29)

The Judgmental Spirit (2:1-5)

When Paul argues in verses 1-5 that the judgmental spirit is inconsistent with proper behavior, he is not simply dealing with insincerity. If we condemn others, should we not ask whether our action contains an element of that fatal pride, that confusion between ourselves and the Creator which is the essence of human sin? Is our despising of others related to our desire to be superior, to play God? If so, we are condemned by the very standard by which we condemn others.

In the face of persons who pretend to be saints but are really committed only to their own self-image, Paul sets forth the very real prospect of a day of judgment in which all of the secrets of the heart will be revealed. He refers several times to the judgment at the end of time in which wrath is a very real possibility.

Paul's contention is that this final judgment will be absolutely impartial. It will evaluate not the level of persons' claims, but rather what they have actually done in this life. This is why in verses 6-10 Paul stresses the absolute fairness of divine judgment. That God is impartial (2:11) means that none of the house churches in Rome can really claim that they have a final corner on the truth. It means that none of us is going to escape an absolutely fair assessment of what we have actually done in this life.

As verses 12-16 make plain, it is not what people say but what they do that really counts. It is not whether people have the right beliefs but whether they manifest that *what the law requires is written on their hearts*. The righteousness of which Paul speaks must be embodied in order to be real.

Judgment According to Works (2:6-7)

One of the most difficult puzzles about Romans 2:6-7 is that these verses appear to contradict the basic teaching of the Reformation which is perceived to be central for Romans, namely, that humans are rightwised by faith alone. Particularly when the thesis of Romans is taken into account (1:16-17), the statement that God will recompense each *according to his works* in 2:6 is quite puzzling. To add to the confusion, verse 13 states that the *doers of the law* shall be rightwised.

Many commentaries attempt to deal with these seeming contradictions by evading the clear force of what Paul says. One approach is to suggest that these verses deal merely with a theoretical possibility. If it is true that all persons sin, then one cannot say that they will be justified according to their works. Paul, for the sake of a theoretical argument, develops here a purely theoretical option. This is a hard argument to sustain in light of the direct references to the Roman audience in 2:5, 7, and 8. We do not gain the impression from these lines that Paul is dealing with something that was not present in Rome.

Another approach is to suggest that Paul is dealing only with Christian believers in this passage. In this way Paul can be seen as condemning non-Christians, but suggesting that those who really have been transformed by the gospel have been rendered capable of producing works and therefore achieving salvation. But the idea that Paul is dealing strictly with a Christian audience in these verses is contradicted by 2:9-10. There the phrase *the Jew first and also the Greek* is repeated.

When Paul uses *work* in the singular, perhaps he has in mind the proper response to God, involving an appropriate faith. Persons capable of achieving this "good work" are those who respond to the truth about God by forming their lives in a faithful and honest manner in imitation of the divine action. Whenever Paul uses *works* in the plural, he has in mind the arrogant, self-justifying works of those who are pretending to be more than they are. Those who do their works as part of the pattern of suppressing the truth about themselves, trying to make themselves look righteous, are on a path that leads towards condemnation. Paul may be opening up the possibility of the righteous Gentile in verses 7 and 13.

This interpretation does not fully resolve the tension

between these verses and the sweeping condemnation of the earlier verses in Romans which suggest that every human without exception tends to suppress the truth about God. Perhaps Paul meant to leave open some loopholes in his earlier argument. Perhaps the statement of the righteous Gentile in Chapter 2 makes it possible for Christians to recognize the occasionally superlative moral achievement of persons outside the Christian faith and even outside of the Judeo-Christian tradition as a whole. These are persons whose lives nevertheless manifest a degree of authenticity and goodness that seems difficult to dispute.

The Relevance of Impartiality (2:8-16)

Recent studies in Romans have made us more aware of the crucial significance of Paul's argument that God does not discriminate between persons, a point which is particularly prominent in 2:11. This is an essential element in the issue of whether God will accept those who have never heard the Christian gospel or the Jewish faith, those who have never heard or perceived the Jewish law but nevertheless perform it (2:13-16).

The idea of God's impartial acceptance of Jews and Gentiles is expanded to imply an aspect of mutual acceptance between the groups themselves. Insofar as the house churches were contending that each had the total truth and that the others were illegitimate, Paul's argument about the impartiality of God stands as a formidable hedge against a competitive spirit. God is not the possession of the "weak" or the "strong."

God is absolutely impartial. God treats persons of all races and nations and religions with an absolutely fair standard of performance. Until the Roman house churches understood this, they would not be able to overcome their tensions and cooperate in a mission to the world. Any gospel they proclaimed to the world would be fatally flawed if it rested on the premise, often assumed in the mission experience of later Christianity, that one group has a corner on the truth and is therefore superior to others. That kind of mission is nothing more than a vicious form of imperialism. Such a gospel was bound to be rejected by the Spaniards, who had already suffered sufficiently from Roman imperialism and would be unlikely to adopt another form.

No Exemption by Religious Status (2:17-29)

The material in verses 17-29 is full of dangers as well as promise. It is particularly dangerous in a culture with a record of some anti-Semitism to discuss Paul's effort to show that Jews as well as Gentiles are involved in sin. Paul's conversation partners here include Jewish Christians in Rome rather than Jews who have not accepted the gospel. We therefore need to assume from the start that this is an argument within the Christian community, not between Christians and unconverted Jews.

Paul hoped to lead the house churches in Rome to a more realistic assessment of their own situation. Those who are convinced that they have earned grace, that they are in a superior position, will never be able to understand the pure gift of grace. Only those who are empty can be filled. Only those who acknowledge their need can be helped. Therefore, this material has a tremendous relevance for the Christian faith. But it can also be dangerous when used in polemic against other religions.

Claims of Religious Superiority (2:17-20)

In verses 17-20 Paul opens up a series of ironic caricatures of claims of religious superiority. The claims that Paul heaps up in these verses were all in use within the Jewish community. To have possession of the Torah and therefore to know God's will and thus be a *light to those who are in darkness* was at the very center of Jewish self-identity. Within the context of understanding one's limitations, there is nothing wrong with this or any of the other attributes Paul lists. To be a teacher of monotheism and a guide to the pagan world was an enviable aspect of Jewish self-identity at the time that Paul was writing. But nowhere else in Jewish literature were all of these claims heaped one upon the other in the way that they are here. Paul's goal was to show that even the finest parts of a national self-identity can become perverse.

This list of the boasts becomes heavier and heavier as it moves towards the end, and finally the sentence collapses without ever being completed. At the very climax of one's boast, the weight of arrogance causes a breakdown. Whenever one's sense of self-identity and responsibility evokes feelings of superiority over others, it collapses under its own weight. It becomes the opposite of what it was intended to be.

Rhetorical Questions (2:21-23)

In verses 21-23 Paul continues with a series of rhetorical questions. Many of these sins were occurring in the Jewish community of the ancient world, just as they are in the Christian community in the modern world. Paul is hoping to evoke a sense of disparity between what one preaches and what one does. His argument had a particular bearing on the conflict among the house churches in Rome. While preaching a gospel of love, they ended up contradicting their beliefs by their actions. Paul presents a rather curious example in the second half of verse 22. There was actually a teaching among the Jewish rabbis that when Jews robbed a pagan temple, they were not stealing but rather "finding" something. Since the pagan gods did not exist, the precious objects in the pagan temple presumably had no owner.

The argument comes to a climax in verse 23 where the basic issue of obeying the law is articulated. It is clear from what we now know about the Jewish world in the first century, however, that this final rhetorical question fit the circumstances of the house churches of Rome far better than it did the Jewish community as a whole. By and large the Jewish community was faithful in its observance to the law and did not find the law a burden at all. In contrast to many Christian stereotypes, there was not a high level of hypocrisy within the Jewish community of the first century. But the same really could not be said for the competing house churches of Rome, which were violating the principle of generous grace by their hardhearted rejection and their polemics against one another. To understand and apply this argument accurately requires us to make a careful translation in terms that would fit our own Christian communities in the twentieth century. Is not the name of God blasphemed because of the way Christian communities have ostracized one another and fought among themselves with techniques that violate the very gospel that they proclaim?

No Exemption Through Circumcision (2:25-29)

Paul moves on in verses 25-29 to deal with the most controversial claim of moral and religious superiority. Circumcision had been under dispute within Christian groups in the seven- or eight-year period before Paul wrote Romans. The opening phase of this dispute is reflected in Acts 15:1 when *some men came down from Judea and were teaching the brethren, "Unless you are circumcised according to the custom of Moses, you cannot be saved."* Paul had struggled over this issue in the apostolic conference (see Galatians 2:1-10), and we have reason to believe that it was an issue also to some degree between the churches in Rome.

Circumcision as the sign of the covenant and the proof of one's membership in the "seed of Abraham" was one of the most important features in the claim of moral and religious superiority on the part of Jewish Christians. That circumcision was perceived by some Christian radicals as necessary for salvation is evident from Acts 15:1, but we have no equivalent indications from the Jewish community that circumcision was assumed to have such relevance.

As far as Jews were concerned, circumcision was simply a sign of adherence and membership in the community of the law. It was faithfulness to this law that insured continuance in the realm of salvation as far as Jewish theology was concerned. But there is no evidence of Jewish theologians in the first century claiming that circumcision was necessary for salvation. It was in the Christian community that circumcision was being used as a sign of superiority of one group over others, evoking Paul's argument in these verses.

Paul's basic contention is that obedience to the law is what makes circumcision significant. The "true Jew" in this sense is the one who has internalized the law of God and obeys it from the heart. The effect of this argument is to make circumcision subordinate to the larger purposes of the law of God.

At the heart of the argument is the contention that the true Jew is the righteous person of any race. Whoever does the will of God from the heart is defined here as the proper Jew. Thus the claims of religious and cultural superiority of Christian groups in Rome are seen to be inappropriate.

§ § § § § § § §

The Message of Romans 2

The major thrust of this passage is that claims of
religious superiority must be abandoned, no matter what
their origin. The major challenge in studying this material
is to avoid falling into anti-Semitic interpretation.

Many commentators perceive Paul to be arguing against
Jews or Judaism in this passage. From the time of the
Reformation down, indeed from virtually the time when
Christianity became the established religion in the Roman
Empire, this has been the major stream of Christian
interpretation. The presumed superiority of Christianity
over Judaism was seen to be the purpose of Paul's
argument. Nothing could be further from the truth. This
kind of interpretation simply leaves intact the very form
of religious superiority that Paul is trying to overcome in
Rome.

The crucial point is that Paul's targets are Christians.
Related to this is the point that the argument is perceived
to be a friendly one. In fact, Paul goes out of his way in
the course of Romans to defend the prerogatives of
Jewish Christians. Paul does not wish to attack Jewish
culture or the Jewish religion. Rather, he wishes to
convince the house churches of Rome that the misuse of
the great religious heritage of the Hebrew Scriptures is
leading to serious disruptions in the life of the
community and to the expression of sinful attitudes and
acts between the Christian groups. When Paul lists the
boasts of the Jews in 2:17-20, he is attempting to
articulate the kind of pride and arrogance that was
surfacing in the Jewish Christian churches in Rome, not
to make a general case against the Judaism of his day.
The "you" in this argument is clearly the Jewish
Christian. This passage can be related to modern
expressions of religious superiority.

Many of the conflicts within denominations in American experience have also witnessed the expression of arguments based on the fallacious claims of religious superiority. People having different views of the inspiration of Scripture or different attitudes toward abortion or toward military service have argued that their own religious perceptions or their own interpretation of Scripture was intrinsically superior to others. It is this kind of situation that Paul's argument in Romans 2 tries to overcome.

§ § § § § § §

Romans 3:1-20

Introduction to These Verses

The previous argument about universal sin raises the
questions that Paul must answer in Romans 3:1-20 to
prove his case. He cannot afford to discredit the Jewish
faith as such, or the Torah on which that faith is based.
He therefore is forced to walk a thin line between
acknowledging the truth of the religious tradition in the
Hebrew Scriptures, while at the same time arguing that
everyone, both Jew and Gentile, is involved in sin in
equal measure.

Here is an outline of Romans 3:1-20.

I. Objections Concerning Universal Sin (3:1-2)
II. The Faithfulness of God (3:3-4)
III. The Fairness of God (3:5-8)
IV. The Question of Jewish Advantage (3:9)
V. The Proof From Scripture (3:10-18)
VI. The Conclusion of the Argument (3:19-20)

An important observation concerning the question-
and-answer style of this material throws light on how it
should be understood. We observed the same kind of
question and answer style in 2:17-22. Many previous
interpreters have understood this as a diatribe against
opponents, an understanding that fit into the prevailing
tradition of an anti-Semitic interpretation of Romans. The
idea of the Jew as the enemy of the Christian lent itself
very easily to this understanding.

Recent research into this question-and-answer style, however, shows that in the Greco-Roman world it was widely used in the grammar school system. The style of the so-called "friendly interlocutor" was frequently used by a skilled teacher in order to discover loopholes in an argument and to build up a case from common sense. The audience was perceived to be friendly in this kind of instruction. This fits closely the circumstances of Paul, who does not wish to confront the Roman Christians as enemies or opponents.

Objections Concerning Universal Sin (3:1-2)

Verses 1-2 take up a serious objection that could easily be raised from the previous argument concerning circumcision. Does Paul really mean that circumcision has no value, that there are no advantages to the Jewish religion? To say yes to these questions is to give up Paul's heritage, indeed, to give up the very source out of which Christianity came.

Above all, as we can see in verse 2, Paul wishes to insist that the great achievement of Judaism is being entrusted with the *oracles* or word of God. The formulation is broad enough that it includes the entire Torah, the prophets, and the writings—the entire Old Testament as understood in the Christian tradition. Since Paul rests his case in Romans so much on citations from the Hebrew Scripture, he does not wish his previous argument to be misunderstood as discrediting the revelation of God in the Hebrew tradition.

The Faithfulness of God (3:3-4)

Even more important from the perspective of Paul's argument in Romans is the issue raised in verses 3-4. If the claims of Jewish superiority are eliminated, can the idea of God's faithfulness be retained?

God had promised to Abraham that his descendants would be as many as the sands of the sea and that the entire Gentile world would be blessed through them. Paul is unwilling to give up the basic idea of God's faithfulness to that promise. Thus he argues in these verses that although some humans have been unfaithful, nevertheless God remains faithful to the promises and will prevail. This is an essential step in the argument concerning the righteousness of God, which is the thesis of Romans (see 1:17). Paul continues this theme by insisting on the fairness of divine judgment. God is not unjust to inflict punishment, because otherwise no judgment or assessment of human behavior at all would be possible. Paul reduces this objection to an absurdity.

The Fairness of God (3:5-8)

In these verses Paul takes up a serious question that any adherent of the Christian faith must think through. Does grace undermine the essential fairness of God? If humans are accepted by grace alone, and if their disobedience is a means by which God's grace and mercy are magnified, how can humans still be condemned?

We see this issue of the fairness of God being dealt with in many of Jesus' parables. Paul carries this line to its most extreme point in 3:8. If humans are accepted by God when they do evil, then why should they cease to do evil? Why not do more and more evil so that God's grace may expand further and further?

This question is more than simply a logical fallacy that Paul wishes to expose. He knew that there were people in the early church who took their freedom in the gospel too far, who fell into libertinism, believing that anything they did could be forgiven. That Christians can do the most sinful things because they are guaranteed of automatic forgiveness is a perversion of the Christian faith. Paul says that it is a slander to charge his theology with that fault. His vehemence on this point is well expressed by the final statement in verse 8, *their condemnation is just.*

The Question of Jewish Advantage (3:9)

Paul moves on to restate the question of Jewish advantage in verse 9. This time he places it in a clearly comparative form: Are they better off than anybody else, than other groups? This is the way the question had to be posed for the Roman house churches, because in fact the Jewish Christian branches were arguing that they were superior to others, just as the Gentile Christian branches were contending for their own superiority. By posing the question this way, the competition is more clearly in view.

In contrast, in Romans 3:1 Paul is simply dealing with the great burden and honor of having received the revelation of God, an honor which bore with it a clear responsibility of humility and service. The question of comparison between one group and the other, however, shifts from the authentic basis of genuine faith, whether Jewish or Christian, and moves into the realm of the sin that Paul describes in Romans 1:18-32.

If the essential sin of humans is to confuse themselves with God and to fall prey to pride, the presence of a competitive spirit between Christian groups was clear evidence that they had already fallen from the position of living their lives entirely on the grace of God to depending on their own achievements.

When Paul asks, *Are we Jews any better off?* it is significant that he includes himself. His own Jewish Christian ancestry, and, by implication, all of the Jewish Christians in Rome, are involved in this question and must face the strong answer, *No, not at all.*

Paul goes on in verse 9 to restate the essential burden of his previous argument, that all persons, including Jews and Greeks, are under the power of sin. Though Paul has not really argued formally for this term *all,* he nevertheless is justified in seeing this as the burden of his argument.

An element of contradiction in his argument still

remains when one reads Romans 2:6 and 13, which show that there are righteous persons of every religion and background who have done the good out of a proper response to the divine will and thus are acceptable to God. But in 3:9 there are no exceptions and no loopholes.

A distinctive Pauline emphasis widely shared by early Christianity is that in light of the cross all persons are seen as sinners. The universal rebellion of the human race is manifest there in the willingness to destroy the best person who ever lived. That reveals a pervasiveness of sin that had never been hinted at in any other previous religious tradition.

The Proof From Scripture (3:10-18)

Paul goes on in verses 10-18 to provide a series of scriptural proofs to the effect that all humans have fallen short of what God expects. It is likely that Paul makes use here of an already-existing list of quotations. The citations are taken out of context, and some of them are altered to fit the new circumstance in a way that was typical for the ancient world. We find the same techniques used by the rabbis and in the Dead Sea scrolls. But the point of Paul's citations is clear: All humans, especially those who claim superiority, are under sin. They show it in their actions. And this is particularly the case with the religious elite. For these citations from the Jewish Scripture are all aimed at the Jewish people themselves, the chosen people from whom sprang several of the groups that were claiming superiority in Rome.

The Conclusion of the Argument (3:19-20)

The conclusion of the first phase of Paul's argument (1:18–3:20) comes in these two verses. Paul insists that every person loyal to the Hebrew Scriptures must accept the judgment that those Scriptures themselves have (3:19). Paul wishes to establish a universal kind of accountability. His hope is to lead the Roman house churches to recognize that no one will be rightwised in God's sight by works of the law.

The thesis that Paul has established in Romans 1:17 comes here to its appropriate development. Until human beings give up the claim that they are superior and righteous in and of themselves, they will not be in a position to understand that God's righteousness comes as a gift, that forgiveness is free, and that faith is the basis of a true life.

In order for the next section of the argument of Romans to be fully understood, 3:20 needs to be understood as foundational. There is a translation problem in using the term *justified* rather than *made righteous* or *rightwised* in the Revised Standard Version and elsewhere. The formulation of this verse relates directly to the thesis of Romans in 1:17.

Paul uses the word in the plural: *works of the law*. He has in mind the kind of works that the Roman house churches were using to prove that they were superior to others. When people do what the law requires for the wrong reasons, performing acts of mercy and keeping a religious community afloat for the purpose of proving their superiority to others, they are condemned.

§ § § § § § §

The Message of Romans 3:1-20

Paul had argued previously about the issue of universal sin. Now he must counter the claims of religious superiority that some groups were making. He does this through the use of the question-and-answer style, a method that is quite appropriate to the argument Paul is constructing.

Paul is dealing here with the most dangerous of Christian vices, self-righteousness. This is the root of Christian arrogance and very frequently the fundamental cause of conflicts between Christian groups. The problem is that persons and groups use their conformity to a certain standard to try to make themselves "righteous." The whole purpose of Paul's argument from 1:18 on is to prove that this cannot work, that this effort in fact is a form of sinful pride, an effort on the part of creatures to make themselves into the Creator, to gain control of their destiny and to dominate others.

Paul is forced to make a very sweeping and hard case, climaxing in 3:20, because he is confronting the kind of conflicts that would later become characteristic of Christian groups, namely self-righteous groups on both right and left claiming their superiority over others, believing that others are damned or lost. They are acting in such a way as to disallow their leadership or their contribution.

Paul's hope is to lead the congregation to see that this terrible perversion of the Christian faith is based on the kind of lie described in Romans 1:25. Whereas the Christian groups in Rome feel certain that they are elect and secure, that they are superior to their competitors, Paul offers a forceful medicine of reality therapy in this argument, ending in 3:20. "No human being can be rightwised in God's sight by works of the law."

If Paul's argument were taken seriously today, it would undercut all claims of cultural or religious superiority, providing a realistic basis for mutual respect between denominations, religions, and nations.

§ § § § § § §

Romans 3:21–4:25

Introduction to These Chapters

This section of Romans contains the final two arguments that support the thesis set forth earlier in Romans 1:16-17. In 3:21-31 Paul states the positive argument concerning humans being rightwised by faith by the one true God. In 4:1-25 Paul sets forth Abraham as the example of such faith and the ancestor of all faithful persons. The key term in these final two sections is *rightwising*, which is often translated as *justification* or *justify*. There are no less than nineteen references to this concept in 3:21–4:25.

Here is an outline of this section.

I. We Are Rightwised by Faith (3:21-31)
   A. Salvation by faith alone (3:21-26)
   B. Righteousness through faith (3:27-31)
II. Abraham as the Example of Faith (4:1-25)
   A. Abraham's faith in God (4:1-8)
   B. Abraham's justification (4:9-12)
   C. Abraham's promise is fulfilled (4:13-22)
   D. The promise to faithful Christians (4:23-25)

The Argument in 3:21–4:25

The abstract quality of Paul's thought often leads people to concentrate on individual sentences rather than on the flow of the argument in this section. This emphasis needs to be qualified by an understanding of the argument as a whole.

In the first phase of the argument, Paul states the major thesis (verses 21-22*a*). Verses 22*b*-26 interpret this thesis, insisting that no distinction can be made between Jews and Gentiles since all have fallen short. Rightwising, therefore, can only be achieved as a gift. This thesis is then proven by a series of traditional, confessional statements regarding the significance of Christ and his redeeming act of life and death.

Salvation by Faith Alone (3:21-26)

In verses 21-28 we come to what has traditionally been called the heart of Romans. It is in this section that Paul's marvelous declaration of salvation by faith alone is stated. Here he proclaims freedom from the performance principle. The righteousness of God in this passage is perceived as God's victory over sin, manifest in the Christ event. This victory transforms humans by making them acceptable to God, despite their failures and despite their rebellion.

The setting right of the human race through Christ conveys to us the grace of God, which we can never earn. This means that our lives are no longer dependent on what we are able to perform, on our obedience to the law. Salvation is understood here as the faithful response of humans to the love of God, manifest in the Christ event.

What has been understood traditionally as "justification by faith" is a matter of being set right by this unconditional love of God, to be restored to the original righteousness that humans were intended to have from the moment of their creation. To stand under this righteousness is to become righteous. It is also understood by Paul as entering the sphere of divine righteousness, that is, submitting to the lordship of Christ. Thus salvation in this passage is more than being turned on. It is more, even, than feeling accepted. It is a matter of submitting to the righteousness of God, which means a change of direction toward the service of God in everyday affairs.

The opposition between law and faith that was stated in the final verse of the previous section (see 3:20) is articulated with the phrase *apart from the law* in verse 21. Paul means that the transformation of the human race does not come through submission to the law, whether this be the law of the Jewish Torah or the laws of one's social group.

The revolutionary quality of the true Christian faith is clearly manifest in this assertion. In most cultures and in many forms of popular Christianity, salvation remains a matter of conforming to certain beliefs or actions. The law takes manifold forms, most of which are not even in the Old Testament. But Paul does not wish to abandon the law except as a cause and means of salvation. He insists that *the law and the prophets bear witness* to the salvation that comes through faith alone. This theme of the Hebrew Scriptures, affirming the doctrine of justification by faith alone, is developed extensively in Chapter 4. But we see evidence of it in the frequent citations from Scripture throughout the Book of Romans.

Paul returns to this important theme in verse 31 when he asks, *Do we then overthrow the law by this faith? By no means! On the contrary, we uphold the law.* Paul is firmly convinced that the law affirms Christ. He contends that we uphold or establish the law by faithfully responding to the final revelation of the law's intent in Christ. But Paul does not mean that we uphold the law in the sense of falling back into conformity. While law can never become a means of salvation, it nevertheless points toward salvation.

In many ways, Paul's formula in verse 24 reveals the central reality of his understanding of salvation. Humans are rightwised *by his grace as a gift*. They do not earn it; indeed they cannot earn it. There is no way that humans can merit a new life, because as Paul has stated in 3:23, all humans without exception sin and *fall short of the glory of God*. We are accepted by God purely on the basis of God's love revealed in the Christ event. Nothing we can ever do will ever earn this.

Paul goes on to refer, in verses 24-26, to a series of abstract approaches to salvation. It is likely that various branches of the early church are being cited in these verses, because each branch had a different terminology and a different way to describe salvation in its hymns and confessions.

One theory is visible in the term *redemption* in verse 24. This term is related to buying the freedom of slaves, releasing them from captivity. We can understand the use for this term for salvation by slaves or freedmen who made up so large a part of the early church. They understood the unconditional love of God as redeeming them.

A second term for atonement is *expiation*, which is used in verse 25. Christians from a Jewish background who were closely associated with the Temple cult would have favored this term, because it refers to the sprinkling of blood on the altar on the day of atonement. Christ achieves forgiveness by shedding his own blood. His death for others was perceived to be the replacement of the Temple cult and the means by which forgiveness is extended to those who do not deserve it.

Expiation is closely related to a third set of terms used in the latter part of verse 25: *This was to show God's righteousness, because in his divine forbearance he had passed over former sins.* For persons who were not associated with the Temple cult, the reality of forgiveness was most clearly expressed with these words. The essence of Christ's life and death was unconditional forgiveness. This restores humans and makes us capable of responding in a positive way to the righteousness of God.

Above all, forgiveness relates to the rebellion that Paul had described in earlier chapters of Romans, which was so manifest in the competition between the Roman house churches.

The fascinating aspect of verses 24-26 is that Paul does not take sides and prefer one of these categories over the other. He seeks to unify the theological options that have divided the church ever since. It is very likely that these three theories were in dispute among the house churches in Rome. But Paul unifies them. He subordinates them to the same categories of the righteousness of God and the rightwising of humans by faith in Christ. These are the common denominators that all three sets of categories shared. The result of this unification effort is that the theological boasting of one side over the other is overcome.

Righteousness Through Faith (3:27-31)

In verses 27-31 the doctrine of righteousness through faith is discussed with questions and answers. If humans can be set right only by faith, their capacity to boast in accomplishments under the law is eliminated. Paul restates the reason for this by formulating the idea of rightwising by faith alone (see verse 27).

In verses 27 and 28, Paul states the underlying reason why law cannot save. Whenever humans become convinced that their life rests on their performance, they inevitably fall into boasting. The competitive spirit comes to the fore as it had in the Roman house churches. That is why Paul must repudiate the principle of works. This leads to what later became the great slogan of the Reformation: We hold that a person is set right by faith apart from works of the law. (See verse 28.)

Faith in this context is the human response to the revelation of the righteousness of God. While it has components of belief, its primary content is loyalty and trust in God's word. Paul is referring not to a set of abstract ideas but rather to a relationship. It is the belief side of the Christian faith which was in dispute in Rome and which was leading the house churches to their vicious struggle against one another. Paul is hoping to unify them by offering an approach to faith that is relational. It is a matter of each person having trust in the Lord, thus submitting to the righteousness of God.

A second topic concerning the priority of Jews and Gentiles is taken up in verses 29-30, where the oneness of God is correlated with the doctrine of the acceptance of Jews and Gentiles by faith alone. When humans attempt to justify themselves by their conformity to the law, they are expressing the age-old human desire to control God. Whenever we make claims that our approach to religion is superior, we are in effect claiming to control God. Paul therefore poses the rhetorical question, *Is God the God of Jews only? Is he not the God of Gentiles also?* Paul holds God to be the God of all people, which means that God's claims are universal and that arrogant religion challenges that claim at the most basic level.

Recent advances in our understanding of Romans make it clear that Paul stressed the oneness of God to counter the exclusive claims of first-century liberals and conservatives. Thus he argued for the inclusion and coexistence of both Jews and non-Jews in the same community, on the basis of faith.

The confession that *God is one* was originally meant to unify the Christian community. The great Hebrew conception of the oneness of God (see 3:30) stands as a bulwark against claims that God is completely encompassed in human formulas. Paul is carrying through here with the idea that we saw in Chapter 1, namely that the essence of human sin is to confuse the creature with the Creator, to worship human institutions and formulas rather than the one true God.

In verse 31 a third brief dialogue is initiated concerning the status of the law. Several points are stated here that are not fully developed until later chapters of Romans, principally Chapter 7.

Abraham as the Example of Faith (4:1-25)

If rightwising comes only through faith, what about the question of being children of Abraham? Did the promise of righteousness not go to him and his descendants? The key thesis that Paul wishes to assert is found in verses 11-12.

Paul makes a case in this chapter that Abraham is the father of the faithful, not of those who obey the law. He thus extends membership in the new Israel beyond racial and religious self-identity.

Abraham's Faith in God (4:1-8)

In verses 1-8, Abraham is shown to be the ancestor of the faithful because he was accepted on the basis of his faith rather than his accomplishments. In this section the primary and secondary texts are developed that dominate the rest of this chapter. The primary text is Genesis 15:6, cited quite accurately from the Septuagint (the Greek version of the Hebrew Old Testament). The secondary text is Psalm 32:1-2, which indicates that the blessing comes only to sinners, to those who have not worked to accomplish the law.

By combining these two texts, Paul extends the blessing that originally came to Abraham and his Jewish descendants to all persons whose iniquities are covered. He therefore makes a case that Abraham is the father of faithful Jews and Gentiles; the common denominator is faith.

Abraham's Justification (4:9-12)

In verses 9-12 the point is made that Abraham's justification occurred prior to the gift of the law and to his own circumcision. Paul uses a rabbinic tradition, based on the Book of Genesis, that circumcision occurred twenty-nine years after Abraham's promise. Faith precedes the law and circumcision is viewed merely as a confirmation of being rightwised by faith.

Abraham's Promise Is Fulfilled (4:13-22)

In verses 13-22 Abraham's promise is shown to have been fulfilled only according to faith. First Paul makes the point that the promise given to him was not bound by law. In verse 15 Paul suggests that since law provides the basis of measuring guilt, it produces wrath instead of life.

Paul construes the faith of Abraham as faith in God, who can create something out of nothing. Abraham believed that God was capable of creating a son even though he and his wife were far past the age when this was physically possible. Abraham's faith, therefore, was in the God *who gives life to the dead and calls into existence the things that do not exist* (4:17). Paul uses a fragment of confessional material in this verse. The rough transition in verse 17, expressed by the dash in the middle of the verse (in the Revised Standard Version) is an indication of the use of liturgical or confessional materials at this point.

The idea of calling into existence the things that do not exist sounds very much like the Creation theology of Hellenistic Judaism and early Christianity, in which God is the one who creates out of nothing. The philosophical interest in the theory of Creation was distinctively Greek. But Paul adapts it here to the Abraham story in a unique way. Abraham's faith is defined as faith in the God who raises the dead. This allows Paul to connect Creation theology with the Christ event as he does explicitly in 4:24-25.

The Promise to Faithful Christians (4:23-25)

Finally, in verses 23-25 Paul correlates salvation by faith alone with belief in the Christ event, in particular, belief in the death and resurrection of Christ. Salvation as experienced by early Christians was itself a new creation. It was experienced as the destruction of an old world and the creation of a whole new self. Under grace, persons were able to acknowledge that their former lives had indeed been nothing, but that God had been able to create out of that nothing, out of that void of sin and depravity, a new life and a new future.

§ § § § § § §

The Message of Romans 3:21-4:25

The key sentence in 4:25 places in nuclear form the connection between the life, death, and resurrection of Christ and the transformation of humans into the new righteousness. Christ died *for our trespasses* in the sense that humans discovered their own hostility against God in the death of Jesus. In that death we recognize the depth of human alienation and sin. But we recognize at the same time that we are forgiven at the very moment of Christ's death. He died for the sake of others, guiltlessly, dying in their places so that they might have communicated to them the surpassing grace of God.

Since Christ was *raised for our rightwising*, Paul is affirming that in the Resurrection the death of Christ was confirmed and the truth of the revelation of Christ was revealed. The theme of dying and rising with Christ that will be developed in Romans 6 receives here its first articulation. Under the power of the Christ event, we recognize that our former lives were null and void. We also see that we have the possibility to share in his resurrection by receiving a new life based on grace rather than on our own accomplishments. For Abraham is indeed the ancestor of the faithful of all generations.

The Creator is capable of producing something out of nothing. This is directly correlated with Christian belief in 4:24, in that Christians believe that God produced life out of the death of Christ. The essence of the Christian orientation, therefore, is to believe that God can make something out of nothing. We humans are nothing; our accomplishments amount to nothing. But God restores us to righteousness by gospel power alone. Faith is defined here as a matter of setting trust in that divine power.

§ § § § § § §

Romans 5

Introduction to These Chapters

The relation of Romans 5:1-21 to the rest of the argument of the letter has been clarified in recent decades. Earlier scholars, under the influence of the Reformation, tended to place this chapter with the first four chapters under the general heading of "justification." We can see the reason for doing this in light of the opening and closing verses of Chapter 5, both of which emphasize rightwising.

Another scheme of dividing Romans was popular in nineteenth-century German scholarship. It tended to place Chapters 6–8 under the heading of a mystical-ethical doctrine of salvation, while placing Chapters 1–5 under the category of a legal doctrine of salvation.

Recent commentators, however, have correctly placed Chapter 5 with the succeeding two chapters. Within this framework, Romans 5:1-11 has an introductory role in the series of amplifications of Paul's basic argument which we find in 5:1–8:39.

In particular, we see themes in 5:12-21, 6:1-23, and 8:1-39 introduced for the first time in this section. The restored relationship with God marked by peace provides the basis for future salvation despite all present sufferings. The paradoxical state of the new life is developed throughout Chapters 5–8, in that the peaceful relationship with God and fellow humans is set in the context of a world in which the principalities and powers are very much present and effective.

In the second half of Chapter 5, Paul sets out the contrasting realms of Adam and Christ.

A number of important themes surface in this chapter: suffering in relation to maturity; peace and reconciliation; the relation between the present experience of rightwising and the future experience of salvation; the cause of human sin and the role of Adam; and the relation between the old age and the new. Christian realism is at the forefront of this passage.

Chapter 5 may be outlined as follows.
I. Introduction to the Argument (5:1-11)
   A. Peace in the midst of affliction (5:1-2)
   B. Afflictions and sufferings (5:3-5)
   C. Reconciliation with God (5:6-10)
   D. Summary statement (5:11)
II. The Realms of Adam and Christ (5:12-21)
   A. Introduction (5:12)
   B. Sin in the garden of Eden (5:13-14)
   C. Adam and Christ are compared (5:15-21)

Peace in the Midst of Affliction (5:1-2)

The passage opens with a succinct summary of the preceding argument from 1:16–4:25. This statement recalls the thesis in Romans 1:17 through the intricate stages of the argument in intervening chapters down to this summary. Being rightwised provides the basis of peace with God, according to the argument of our new section.

Before there can be peace, however, there must have been war. It is impossible to understand the argument of Chapter 5 without recalling the extensive argument that Paul has laid out up to this point, that human beings had indeed declared war on God and that this war had been overcome by the cross and resurrection of Christ.

The rebellion of humans by suppressing the truth about the distinction between themselves and God, with its dreadful consequence of the distortion of all human life, is the presupposition of this chapter. When God forgives humans and accepts them by grace alone, the necessity for their rebellion is eliminated. We no longer have to prove ourselves. We no longer have to compete. We no longer have to play God. This is what Paul means by the gift of peace. We can stand in a firm relationship *with God through our Lord Jesus Christ* (5:1), because we are no longer attempting to play God and to resist the truth.

The content of this peace is described in 5:2 in terms of *access to this grace in which we stand.* Paul refers here to the love of God conveyed to human beings through Christ who accepts us as we are. This grace enables a new relationship, so that the task of Christian faith is to stand firmly on that relationship rather than falling back into some form of self-righteousness.

This argument had a particular significance for the Roman house churches, which were competing with one another in a situation of virtual warfare. Paul does not wish to imply, however, that our peace with God and with fellow Christians means the difficulties of life have been resolved. This would produce a shallow, unrealistic faith incapable of dealing with the real world. Thus Paul contrasts the firm relationship in which we stand with the future hope of *sharing the glory of God.* Such glory is going to be manifest at the end of history.

Afflictions and Sufferings (5:3-5)

In the meantime, there are sufferings that must be endured. The Roman churches had experienced such afflictions and sufferings in various ways, and in some sense were experiencing them in the present time with the return of the refugees and the difficulties that they were finding in relocating and finding places in the churches that they had left.

Paul himself has experienced more than his share of

sufferings in his missionary travels. It is the presence of the old age with its suffering and trouble that makes for the necessity of hope (5:1, 5). The peace that Paul has in mind, therefore, is a dynamic, forward-looking one, requiring hope for its fulfillment.

Some have inferred from reading verses 3-5 that Paul was something of a masochist who offers a positive justification for suffering. He does not, in fact, suggest that suffering comes from God or is particularly to be welcomed. Instead, he suggests that the Christian is able to rejoice in sufferings because he or she is sure of God's love (5:5).

Within this context, sure of God's love, no suffering can separate us. And when we hope in the future fulfillment of God's plan, suffering can be received positively. It is within this context that Paul suggests that suffering produces endurance. To gain such positive benefits from suffering requires the foundation of the love of God and the peace with God who sustains us during troubles.

Reconciliation With God (5:6-10)

In verses 6-10 Paul moves on to set forth his powerful doctrine of reconciliation. The premise of this section is that humans are in fact *sinners* (verse 8) and *enemies of God* (verse 10).

Paul develops this basic idea in a somewhat awkward manner, developing a comparison in verse 7 which he has to qualify in the second half of that verse. The basic point is easy to understand: God conveys love to humans despite their rebellion by means of Christ dying for the ungodly.

In verses 9-10 Paul lays out the basis for the hope of future salvation. While Paul speaks of reconciliation and rightwising as a current or past experience, he consistently in this chapter reserves salvation for the future. We encounter this for the first time in 5:2, where participation in the glory of God is placed in the context of future hope rather than present experience. We see this even more clearly in verses 9 and 10, where rightwising and reconciliation are contrasted with the future salvation. We encounter the same kind of contrast in 5:17 and 6:8.

Paul probably makes a distinction between present suffering and future fulfillment in order to insert a note of realism into early Christian enthusiasts. These people believed that, with the dawn of the new age and the gift of the spirit, they were already participating in the resurrected life. This would imply that troubles would be completely eliminated and that evil had been overcome.

Paul's contention in 5:1–8:39 is that the Christian life must be lived out against the threats of a still-fallen world. He does not wish to deny that regeneration has already occurred and that the new life is presently available. What the *reservation* implies, however, is that the fulfillment is yet to come. The Christian life makes no sense in the context of troubles and afflictions without the principle of hope. Any Christian who loses sight of this will remain terribly vulnerable in times of persecution and natural disaster. The *peace* that we have with God sustains us through persecution and trouble but does not relieve us from them. Salvation in the final sense is a future hope for Paul.

Summary Statement (5:11)

This argument is summarized in verse 11, where the present rejoicing in God centers in the firm relationship that has been established through Christ. Reconciliation is a reality no matter what troubles this world may lay upon us. In the conclusion of this sentence, the themes that will be dealt with through the rest of the next three chapters are stated. Not until the end of Chapter 8 will Paul return and offer the resolution of the problem of remaining faithful as well as hopeful in a world where evil continues at times to predominate.

The Realms of Adam and Christ (5:12-21)

With 5:12-21, Paul opens up some of the most provocative and highly debated topics in his letter—the origin of sin and the relation between the realm of Christ and the realm of the fallen world.

Introduction (5:12)

In verse 12, a paradoxical thesis is stated. Like several of the other heavy sentences in Romans, this one remains incomplete. The first portion of this sentence stands firmly within the tradition of the Adam speculation of ancient Judaism. This concept suggests that evil came into the world through the first man and woman, and that the fate of the subsequent inhabitants of this globe was decisively determined by the actions of their ancestors.

This deterministic picture, however, is altered with the final words of verse 12 in which the contradictory viewpoint is suddenly stated: *because all men sinned*. Paul states the paradoxical view that humans are all responsible for their deeds regardless of what Adam did. According to Paul, each human being sins in his or her own behalf. Here we have, side by side, two paradoxical sides of the doctrine of sin, the one deterministic, and the other voluntary. Paul means to hold both of these views in tension.

Paul is trying to hold together here doctrines that have been perceived to be absolutely opposed to one another, not only in ancient Judaism but in modern thought as well. Paul holds the view that both sides of this antithesis seem equally true. This paradox needs considerable discussion, because for the most part Christians have tended to take one side or the other, but rarely have they taken both sides.

Sin in the Garden of Eden (5:13-14)

In these verses, Paul reviews the traditional teaching of the sin of the first humans in the garden of Eden. He refers to this sin repeatedly as the effort to become like God. In these verses Paul contends that sin preceded the giving of the law, following in this regard Jewish theology of the ancient period as well as the biblical record.

In order to understand this argument, some perspective must be provided for the figure of Adam. While many people in the ancient world conceived of Adam as a historical figure, he is used here more in the sense of an archetype. He is the figure that does what others later do, functioning therefore as a kind of pattern.

Many modern people are more comfortable with understanding the Adam figure as a mythical narrative than as a historical account. As history, the story of the first man and woman causes problems with modern science. But as story, as true story, it reveals the depth of the human dilemma. The Adam figure continues to exercise a profound influence on the human mind.

Adam and Christ Are Compared (5:15-21)

In the rest of Chapter 5 Paul develops an elaborate series of comparisons between Adam and Christ, the one clearly a historical figure, the other a kind of abstract pattern. But both exercise a very real power: Adam in a sense ruling the fallen world, and Christ offering a new existence under grace. Behind the contrast between Adam and Christ stands the long tension between the church and the world, the old age and the new.

In the five elaborate comparisons, Paul succeeds in setting forth the distinctive shape of the new age, marked by grace, the free gift, rightwising, life, acquittal, obedience, righteousness, and grace. The old age, in contrast, is marked by the trespass, judgment, condemnation, death, disobedience, and sin.

Paul thought it necessary to develop this contrast at length in order to make plain that the life of righteousness is lived out next to the realm of unrighteousness. Paul thinks of the world as dramatically shaped by two power spheres, the sphere of sin and the sphere of Christ. Each has its ethos and each has its adherents. The life of affliction that is to be lived in faith must take the realm of Adam seriously.

In the final two verses of Chapter 5, the themes are stated for the succeeding chapters. In verse 20, Paul deals with the issue of law coming in to increase the trespass. This topic is developed extensively in Chapter 7. In verse 21 he deals with the realm of grace reigning through righteousness which states the major theme for Chapter 6, the new life in Christ.

Paul's over-arching theme, therefore, is that grace is victorious over sin. Christ's realm is greater than Adam's realm. This is what gives Paul the capacity to respond to suffering in a positive way and to remain hopeful about the future of the mission of God's word.

§ § § § § § §

The Message of Romans 5

In Chapter 5 we encounter one of the pervasive themes in Pauline theology, namely the overlapping of the two ages. The age of Adam, marked by sin and death, is counterpoised against the sphere of Christ, marked by rightwising and life. Particularly from verses 15-17, we gain the sense of these two ages in tension, with Christians caught between. We are members of Christ's age but still conscious of the pervasive impact of the old world.

This feature of Pauline thought has manifested itself throughout Romans. His very mission plan to go to Spain seems to have been shaped by this sense of end-time urgency. The thesis of Romans, that the righteousness of God is revealed at the present time, strongly suggests the dawning of a new age. The hope expressed in this passage of the glory of God being manifested in believers breathes the spirit of the fulfillment of history toward which Paul was working.

The overlapping of the ages produces an element of tension which is crucial to understanding Pauline thought.

This vital sense of life as a constant struggle is what provides the element of realism that we detect from the opening lines of Chapter 5 and which will be the major theme to be traced through the end of Chapter 8. Evil is a reality. The old world is still in effect, even though the new world has dawned. The frequent use of battle metaphors in Christian hymns speaks to this underlying truth, that the Christian life of righteousness involves a struggle for righteousness. It involves a constant battle against the old age.

§ § § § § § §

Romans 6

Introduction to These Chapters

In Romans 6 we encounter a passage that bristles with difficulties. A glance through the standard commentaries will reveal a series of theological land mines strewn throughout the wording of this powerful passage. This is where the question of perfectionism and sanctification has been argued, an issue crucial for the holiness movement and for Wesleyan theology. Those who strongly oppose a perfectionist theology, stressing that humans remain sinners even after becoming Christians, find much that needs restatement or adjustment in this chapter.

The chapter also includes the most explicit statement in Paul's letter to the Romans relating to the sacraments, in this case of baptism. Yet baptism is handled in this passage in a way that allows the passage to be used even by people who have a rather non-sacramental view of the Christian faith.

Finally, this chapter has the clearest statements of what has been called Christ-mysticism in Pauline thought. Since many theologians are skeptical of mystical theology, substantial efforts have been made to readjust what Paul says on this issue as well.

Yet with all of these problems, there are powerful resources for faith in this chapter. Paul's contention is that the old Adam does not prevail. The new life is a reality. Humans are set free from sin and have a relationship in Christ. This is the good news at the heart of Romans.

Romans 6 has three main parts.

I. Sin and Baptism (6:1-14)
II. Sin and Lordship (6:15-20)
III. The Issue of Sanctification (6:21-23)

The Flow of the Argument

In Romans 6 Paul continues to deal with the implications and objections concerning his doctrine of the righteousness of God. In verse 1 he takes up the question that arose from the last verse of Chapter 5, that grace abounds more than the increase of sin. Verse 2 answers this question emphatically by stating the inconsistency of living in the realm that has just been overcome, the realm of sin.

Verses 3-7 explain this principle of inconsistency, showing that in baptism believers have experienced the death of Christ and are set free to participate in a new life with Christ. The theme of life runs through Chapter 6, with a particular emphasis on living as agents of divine righteousness.

The conclusion of the argument in verse 14 states the proper relation of grace to law, by maintaining the incapacity of sin to reign over those in Christ.

In verses 15-23, Paul raises the question that was discussed in the final verse of the preceding section. If believers are *not under law but under grace*, why, then, is there any necessity for moral urgency? This question is answered on the basis of the idea of exchanging lordship, first stated in verse 16. Salvation is understood as being redeemed from an evil lord and made the servant of another.

Verses 17-20 provide an expansion of this basic idea, contrasting the new lordship with the old. Verses 20-23 lift up the consequences of the two lordships, the one leading to shame and death and the other leading to holiness and life.

Sin and Baptism (6:1-14)

In verses 1-14 we encounter the question and answer form of argument once again. This section deals with a basic issue for the Christian faith: Is there a real difference between our life in the old age and our life in the new? Is the realm of sin still dominant in the world? The behavior of the Christians at times makes it appear that nothing in fact has changed. But in Paul's view, that jeopardizes the triumph of the gospel of Christ.

Paul opens with the question of whether sin remains dominant: Should we *continue in sin that grace may abound*? (verse 1). Paul forcefully denies this option and states in the second half of verse 2 the basic inconsistency. If one has died to the realm of sin, how can one *still live in it?*

When the church acts like the world, Paul suggests, it is being inconsistent with the new age, unresponsive to grace. This point had a very direct relevance for the Roman house churches and for modern churches as well. Although sin frequently occurs within the church, it is not inevitable. It is, in fact, a fundamental denial of the new life in Christ.

In verses 3-7, the issue of inconsistency is explained in light of an experience that the Roman Christians had undergone—baptism. It is clear that Paul was dealing with persons who, for the most part, had not been baptized as infants. Most of them probably had undergone baptism as adults in response to the basic transformation that the gospel had produced.

What is striking in Paul's interpretation of baptism, however, is its relational character. The ceremony is not perceived as having any magical force. It embodies instead a new relationship. Paul describes this relationship with a variety of powerful expressions.

In verse 3 there is a reference to being baptized *into his death*. That is, the gospel convinces people that Christ died for them and that his death was one that they had deserved. In light of the cross, they discovered their own hostility against God, their own guilt that was worthy of death. But simultaneously in the gospel they discovered that Christ had suffered that death for them, and they realized that his death was their own. Thus baptism is an indication of their identification with Christ.

Similarly, in Romans 6:4 there is a reference to being *buried* with him through baptism into death, so that personal union with Christ is at the center of the understanding of baptism. In verse 5, Paul refers to being *united with him*, or perhaps "fused together in the likeness of his death." These vivid expressions of personal identification and relationship are designed to show that a very real change is wrought by the gospel. This change is described in verse 6 in terms of the death of the old, self-centered person bound by the sin and compulsions that marked our former lives.

When Paul refers to the *sinful body* that is destroyed in baptism, he does not mean that the physical body is itself repressed or placed under bondage. Rather, he means that the old self that had been dominated by sin was destroyed. The rule of sin has been broken. The gospel conveys to us a realization of the depth of our hostility against God, while at the same time conveying our unconditional acceptance. When we discover that we are made right by God's grace alone and that our deepest anxieties are allayed, we are freed from the compulsions toward a self-centered life.

In verses 8-11, Paul reaffirms the new relationship as the key to the new life. We now *live with him* just as *we have died with Christ* (verse 8). Just as Christ lived a life in relation to God, so we now should view ourselves as *alive to God in Christ Jesus* (verse 11).

The new relationship is the mark of the new life. We no longer serve the powers of the old age. Thus the exhortations in verses 12 and 13 are to live out the new relationship. The thesis of Romans is thus carried through as humans become *instruments of righteousness* (verse 13).

In Romans 6, Paul clearly and explicitly reserves the believers' participation in the resurrection to the future (6:5, 8). It is, in fact, characteristic in Paul's authentic letters that he always sets the resurrection in the future (see Philippians 3:10, 21). In contrast, the later epistles speak of current participation in the resurrected state: *You were buried with him in baptism, in which you were also raised with him through faith in the working of God* (Colossians 2:12; see also Ephesians 5:14).

It is hard to deny that in Romans 6 substantial elements of mysticism are present. Paul does have a kind of personal relationship with Christ which is very intense and real. This relationship correlates closely with Paul's intense prayer life and his expectation that the life of the believer should pattern itself after the life of Christ (see verses 10-11). But it is important to keep in mind that the kind of physical mysticism that is part of the Pauline tradition is also a kind of historical mysticism. Paul places the believer in the context between the death and resurrection of Christ, which is a past event, and the resurrection, which is a future event.

Those who wish to grasp the distinctive contours of Pauline mysticism, therefore, must take pains to differentiate it from traditional mysticism. Normally in a mystical theology, one is united with the divine force so that a kind of union is achieved. This sometimes involves a loss of personal identity as a person is absorbed into the divine realm.

A second distinctive feature of traditional mysticism is the loss of temporality. In mystical experience one may feel freed from time, reunited with past or future figures and events. Time, in such an experience, seems to stand still or to be irrelevant. One has the sense of participating in divine time or in timelessness.

In both of these regards Pauline mysticism is very different. Rather than a fusion between the believer and Christ there is rather a kind of marriage, a relationship in which Christ remains Lord and in which the believer remains the servant. Furthermore, far from being abolished, time in Pauline mysticism is enhanced in its importance. Romans 6 anchors the believer securely in this world between the death and resurrection of Christ in the past, and the triumph of righteousness at the end of time.

The frequent shifts between present, past, and future verbs make this anchoring in time a distinctive and unusual feature of Pauline mysticism. There is also little of the expected kind of inactive contemplation in Pauline mysticism. The result of baptism when properly understood is that Christians view themselves as *instruments of righteousness* (verse 13) whose task is to yield their *members as slaves of righteousness unto holiness* (verse 19). The ethical dimension of the Christian life is completely fused with Pauline mysticism in these verses.

Sin and Lordship (6:15-20)

The diatribe, or question-and-answer style of argument, is used again at the beginning of the second section of Romans. The question springs from a possible misunderstanding of the final verse of the preceding section. If we are not under law, what keeps us from sin? What provides the new form of self-control? Should we simply follow our whims?

This was a very relevant question, because the "weak" Christians in Rome believed that the law remained as an essential element of self-control, whereas the "strong" were arguing that freedom from the law meant Christians were free to do what they pleased.

Paul answers the question about sinning under grace with the concept of the exchange of lordship. Throughout this section he uses the idea of the lordship of Christ that was expressed in the early Christian confession, "Jesus is Lord."

Humans face a choice, whether to serve sin or

righteousness (verse 16). In verses 17-20, the two types of lordship are contrasted. The argument begins not with a warning, however, but with a word of thanksgiving. Paul is convinced that sin is not inevitable. We can choose our master. We can rest our lives on the new relationship, as verse 17 points out. That new relationship responds to the gospel, described as *a type of teaching to which you were given.*

But we face an either-or choice, according to verse 18. Paul acknowledges the difficulty of referring to Christians as being *slaves of righteousness.* It was especially problematic for the "strong" in Rome, who stressed Christian freedom and probably would have been offended by this formulation. But Paul does not shrink from returning to his case after the brief apology at the beginning of verse 19.

In verses 19*b*-20 he develops the basic idea of the tension and the contrast between the two realms. The terms *impurity and iniquity* are contrasted to *righteousness and sanctification.* This emphasis does not mean that Paul abandons his commitment to Christian freedom, as we will see in 8:15 where he denies that believers have been given a servile disposition in Christ. But here in Chapter 6 the emphasis is that serving is not a take-it-or-leave-it affair. We are under a new lordship. And if we refuse the requirements of that new lordship, we simply fall back into the old bondage to sin.

The exhortation in verses 19-20 is to live out the requirements of the new life. The wording of these verses had a very direct relevance for the Roman house churches which were living in a contradiction, and needed to make a choice between these two forms of lordship.

The Issue of Sanctification (6:21-23)

The seriousness of the choice between the two forms of lordship is affirmed by the contrasts between life and death in verses 21-23. Here the argument of Chapter 5 is applied. Christians constantly face a choice between Adam and Christ, and if they choose Adam, they choose death. There is no middle ground. We are caught between the old versus the new and death versus life.

The result of Paul's argument is that there is no new life without holy servanthood. If we do not bear live lives of holiness (verse 22), we are not part of the new age.

Although this theme of sanctification is fundamental for the entire chapter, it has been very difficult to grasp. For centuries Protestants have tended to separate justification and sanctification. They viewed justification as the beginning of the Christian life and sanctification as its consequence or verification. One result of this distinction is that sanctification is viewed as secondary, as a kind of add-on to the Christian life.

A related problem is that justification was understood to be the result of grace much more than sanctification was. The door was left open for sanctification to be understood as a human effort to conform oneself to the new law of God. Since this view so easily resulted in a new and devastating form of legalism, some Protestant thinkers downplayed sanctification and denied that it was possible or even feasible. The well-known Lutheran formula, "simultaneously justified and a sinner," was often understood to mean that no real sanctification was ever possible. Salvation was thus defined in Protestant orthodoxy as having the proper belief while the issue of proper behavior was relegated to the secondary realm.

Some features of Paul's argument in Romans 6 serve to counter some of the negative tendencies of the traditional approach towards sanctification. One of them is that Paul understands sanctification as the natural result of the exchange of lordship. Holiness is not understood as a merely human activity, the result of humans following high ideals. In verse 19 there is an explicit reference to *slaves of righteousness unto holiness*. Here the rightwising activity of God is understood to be fused with sanctification, both of which come to those who submit themselves to the gospel.

The union between justification and sanctification is even more firmly secured by our current understanding of justification as "rightwising," in which the righteous control of God over the entire world is possible. That humans could be rightwised without having their lives altered is inconceivable for Paul. This fact helps us understand the central thrust of Romans 6, that Christians cannot content themselves with a life under sin after they have been made part of the new age.

Sanctification for Paul is therefore not a human achievement. It is the gift that comes from a new relationship with God. Sanctification is closely related to the task of Christian believers to yield their *members to God as instruments of righteousness* (verse 13).

For Paul, response to the gospel implies that one becomes a member of the realm of righteousness and promotes righteousness in everyday life. Sanctification must be united with rightwising if Romans 6 is to be properly understood.

§ § § § § § §

The Message of Romans 6

Paul is realistic in this chapter. He believes that the
Christian life is poised between dying and rising. The
baptism that we experience does not abolish the ravages
of time. Rather, it places Christians in a formative
relationship to past and future events. The past event is
the death and resurrection of Christ; the future event is
the return of Christ at the end of time and the final gift
of glory.

We live between the times, which inserts an undeniable
element of tension within the Christian life. It keeps us
from ever being satisfied with things as they are, and
particularly with our own performance. It counters our
tendency toward over-confidence.

The death and resurrection of Christ in the past and
the coming triumph of righteousness are the definitive
poles of Christian self-identity, far more real to believers
than the news events that pour over our consciousness
day by day or the trends that our popular prophets
perceive.

This tension between faith and world produces a
certain skeptical attitude on the part of Christians
concerning the world around them. Early Christians had
a clear sense of not being defined by the world. One of
the reasons they were persecuted was that they seemed
constantly to be marching to a different drummer, to
have a different sense of time. They were, in fact, poised
between dying and rising, caught and enlivened by the
tension between the already and the not yet. Thus they
were tough, resilient, and forward-looking. They walked
with clear eyes through a world that they knew was
obeying a false god. But they were perfectly confident,
despite all setbacks and persecutions, of the future that
they had to share.

The *eternal life* referred to in 6:22-23 is an integral part of this robust consciousness. The early Christians realized that while they were already participants in this eternal life, they were still living in a dying world. They already had the *free gift of God* (verse 23). But they recognized that nothing they accomplished in this life would ever be complete until the end of time.

§ § § § § § §

Romans 7

Introduction to This Chapter

In this chapter, Paul turns to a topic that had been touched on repeatedly earlier in the argument of Romans. In the last chapter we read what he had to say about not being under law but under grace (6:14-15). Earlier we encountered Paul's idea of the law increasing the trespass (5:20). Before that, we heard of the law bringing wrath (4:15) and that *through the law comes knowledge of sin* (3:20).

In this chapter, Paul reaffirms the basic idea of Christians being released from the law (7:6), answering several important objections that could have led to a misunderstanding of Paul's basic idea. He offers a revolutionary perspective on the law, seen in the light of the Christ event, and of Paul's own experience from his conversion through his struggles with the law in the early church.

Each of the issues in Romans 7 had a direct relevance to the Roman house churches. Thus, although the argument appears somewhat abstract and general in places, it had a very practical bearing on the problems being faced by the congregations in Rome.

Chapter 7 may be outlined as follows.

I. The Two Ages and the Law (7:1-6)
II. The Problem With the Law (7:7-12)
III. Sin and Paul's Conversion (7:13-25)

The Flow of the Argument

The argument in Romans 7 can be divided into three parts. Verses 1-6 describe life in Christ as freedom from the law. This section takes up the theme of the law that was announced in 6:14. The idea of an exchange of lordship or jurisdiction from Chapter 6 is stated in the form of this question in 7:1.

Verses 2-3 develop the analogy of the marriage law to establish the point that jurisdiction does not continue after death has occurred. Verses 4-6 then apply this principle to Christians who have died to the law in experiencing this shift in lordship through Christ. Under Christ, a new relationship in the spirit is established.

The second section, verses 7-12, answers an objection concerning the law that arises out of Paul's formulation in 7:5. His reference there to the *sinful passions* being *aroused by the law* could easily lead to the objection that law now falls into the moral status of sin. This is the false conclusion that Paul denies in Romans 7:7, and then goes on to explain with the idea of the law making humans conscious of sin.

Verses 8-11 elaborate on this idea, showing that sin merely found an *opportunity* in the law, leading to covetousness and death. This section is concluded in verse 12, reaffirming the point that the law is holy and good.

The third section, verses 13-25, answers an objection that could arise from Paul's references to the deceit of the law in verse 11 and the goodness of the law in verse 12. The question in verse 13 deals with the effect of the law on humans. Paul's thesis is that sin invaded the law to produce death. This thesis is sustained by the argument in verses 14-23, showing how sin prevents a person from achieving the desired good. This argument is followed by the statements of verses 24-25 about the wretchedness of the human plight through Christ. The final half of verse 25, then, summarizes the argument.

The Two Ages and the Law (7:1-6)

In this section Paul develops a comparison between marriage law and the situation of Christians standing between the two ages. The point of the comparison is that once the husband dies the woman is free from the marriage contract.

Paul argues in the conclusion of this section (verses 4-6) that the law has jurisdiction only in the old age, and that those who belong to the new are comparable to the woman whose husband has died. She is free, and so are those who had formerly been held under bondage to the law. The phrase *in the flesh* (verse 5) refers to the status of persons in the old age. They are shaped by self-seeking and the kind of sinful self-will that is characteristic of Paul's use of flesh in a context like this.

The question of freedom from the law as a mark of the new age plays a role in the conflict that has been discerned between the weak and the strong in Rome. In all probability, the conservatives were arguing that the Jewish law continues its jurisdiction in the new age. The thrust of Paul's argument at this point is clearly on the side favored by the strong, namely that with the dawn of the new age, the law no longer has jurisdiction. But at the end of verse 6, Paul makes it clear that members in the new age continue to *serve*, not in the old way, bound by the law, but in the new ethical situation of being bound to Christ.

The crucial question for Paul is, Whom does one serve? He cannot conceive of persons not serving; absolute freedom in the sense that some modern people imagine it was not even a possibility for him. As we discover in the modern world, living lives of absolute freedom is not possible for us, either.

The Problem With the Law (7:7-12)

When Paul refers to freedom *from the law* (7:6), the assumption is that he wished to free Christians from the law of the Pharisees or of the Old Testament. The reformers, as well as Wesley and many modern interpreters, have assumed that the problem with the law was its complication and the fact that it was impossible to obey in its entirety. To be saved by grace, according to this interpretation, was to be forgiven for those failures. The law, in that sense, functioned primarily in a negative manner. It showed persons where they had failed to obey. Its function was to evoke guilt feelings.

There is no evidence whatsoever that Paul had experienced difficulty in obeying the law before his conversion, or that he had guilt feelings that were resolved by his conversion. That mistaken interpretation really began with Augustine and developed in its final form in Luther. Luther taught that the law was impossible to obey with sincerity and precision, and that its major function was to impose a burden of guilt on human beings so that they could be driven to rely on grace. Those who failed to acknowledge this fell into self-righteousness, which was the final form of sin. But whether the problem was weakness or self-righteousness, the task of Christians was presumably to probe their conscience and recognize how far they had fallen short.

When Paul describes his previous life, it is clear that he felt he had been entirely successful in obeying the law. Paul clearly felt that the Jewish law in all its complication was perfectly capable of being obeyed, and that indeed since the time he shouldered the burden of the law at the age of thirteen, he had not failed a single time. This is what the term *blameless* means (see Philippians 3:6).

A second major factor leading to a revision of the traditional view is the discovery that in the Judaism of Paul's time there was in fact no assumption that the law was difficult or impossible to obey. A widely-accepted assessment among scholars today is that most loyal Jews carefully observed the law in Paul's time, despite all the complications of its requirements. The gift of the law was viewed as a great benefit. It was a privilege to obey.

Joy in performing the law was expressed when faithful Jews repeated this blessing as they performed the most minute commandment: "Blessed be thou, O Lord, who has sanctified us with thy commandments and has commended us."

This insight leads to a reconsideration of what Paul had in mind when he speaks in Romans 7:5 of our *sinful passions* being aroused by the law, leading to death. Paul goes on to describe how sin invades and corrupts the law (see verses 7-8). The stress on coveting as the essence of sin is closely related to what Paul understands by sinful passions. The problem is not in obeying the law, but in what humans hope to get out of such obedience. The yearning to control our life by our own effort, to remain at the center of the world, is at stake here.

Paul uses the example of coveting in verse 8 because this desire to be at the center of the world and to control one's destiny is linked to what Paul had earlier referred to as the essence of sin. The problem with the law, in short, is that our conformity to its expectations is so frequently used for the purposes of prideful control. This, in fact, was what occurred in the Roman house church situations, where the conformity of the various groups to their sense of religious obligation was used in an aggressive way to prove their superiority over others and to exclude others. This is why Paul identifies sin as the agent that leads to the corruption and the perversion of the law. Sin leads humans to misuse the law, resulting in their own death.

Sin and Paul's Conversion (7:13-25)

In verses 13-25, Paul describes the bondage that leads humans to do the opposite of what they truly desire to do. For generations, Christians have tended to believe that Paul was describing his (allegedly) frustrated, guilt-ridden life in Judaism in these verses. On the

mistaken premise described above, namely that the
Jewish law was impossible to obey, the notion that Paul
lacked the willpower to obey the law has been read into
this passage. Paul is thus viewed as the person who
desired to do the law but was incapable of achieving it
fully, therefore falling into guilt.

The disparity between Paul's high ideals and his actual
performance was then thought to be described in these
verses. But this interpretation has had to be eliminated
because of a new understanding of how the law was
actually viewed in Paul's day. The former understanding
contradicts Paul's own description of his flawless behavior
prior to his conversion.

A new kind of contradiction needs to be sought out
that explains the connection between verses 13-25 and
Paul's former life. Paul's conversion, in fact, was directly
related to his own perfect conformity to the law.

Paul had been convinced that the followers of Jesus
who had broken free from the law should be killed, or
forced back into conformity. He opposed the Jesus
movement because it liberated people from conformity to
the law and because its leader, Jesus of Nazareth, had
been executed as a lawbreaker. What Paul discovered on
the Damascus Road was that Jesus the sabbath breaker
was Jesus the Messiah. His appearance to Paul on the
road proved that he was indeed resurrected as the
disciples were claiming.

The Resurrection meant that everything Jesus taught
and lived and died for was confirmed by God. In an
instant full of grace, Paul discovered the truth about
himself and about conformity to the law in general. He
discovered that his own conformity, his own perfect
obedience to the law, contained within itself a profound
hostility against God. In his zeal for the law, Paul was
supporting the crucifixion of the Messiah and the
persecution of the followers of Jesus.

What Paul discovered, in short, was that sin can hide

itself in the midst of religious conformity. When he writes that *I do not do what I want, but I do the very thing I hate* (verse 15), Paul is describing the profound dilemma of his former life. He had sought to do the will of God and had passionately devoted himself to conformity to the law. But he found that he ended up in hostile reaction against God.

The cross event revealed to Paul the deepest dilemma of the human heart. The very person who is most devoted to conforming himself or herself to the will of God can end up in an unconscious revolt against God. This is the final dimension of the truth that humans *suppress*, according to 1:18-32.

Fleshliness and Sin (verse 14)

What is the cause of this dilemma that seems to afflict humans when they least expect it? Paul's answer is stated repeatedly through the seventh chapter of Romans, but the statement in verse 14 is especially important: *I am carnal, sold under sin.*

Paul is often misunderstood at this point, particularly because of the way he uses *flesh* (*carnal*, in the Revised Standard Version) in this verse and the term *members* in verse 23. Often these references are connected to the so-called "lower nature" of human beings. Flesh comes to be identified with sexuality and with sensual temptations of various sorts. When this interpretation is followed, the human plight is understood to be the one described by the Greeks, presuming the pull of the lower nature against the higher side of the mind. Recall the image of the sailors tying Ulysses to the mast as they sailed past the sirens, because the pull of the passions would otherwise overpower him.

Paul had nothing of this sort in mind. He refused to divide humans between mind and body. He held firmly to the Judaic tradition that the body is good and that sexual desires have their proper place in God's world.

The important clue is that Paul connects flesh with sin throughout this passage. And sin should not be defined in this context as sensuality. As defined in earlier sections of Romans, sin is human rebellion against God.

Often we are able to suppress the knowledge of our deeds and their deepest motivation, Paul suggests. We are unconscious of the universal human tendency to try to be invulnerable, standing alone at the center of the world. The use of *sin* in Chapter 7 indicates that it is self-righteousness and pride that comprise the human dilemma. It is the desire to boast about our own accomplishments that corrupts us. It is the pride that our insights are superior to someone else's, that we desire more prestige than they. This is what led Paul before the Damascus experience to hold so firmly to his own view of the law that he was able and willing to persecute those that were free from it.

Weakness and Self-Righteousness (verse 15)

A widespread misinterpretation of Paul's concept of flesh and body concentrates on the issue of weakness. In this verse, flesh symbolizes the inability of persons to achieve their high ideals. This approach was particularly popular in Puritan and post-Puritan thinkers, and it played a major role in American education. Whenever we say that we know what is right but we do not have enough willpower to do it, we are following this particular line of interpretation from Romans 7.

This interpretation has expressed itself in two different theories about Paul. The first is the idea of the weakness of the Jews in obeying the law. This was followed by Luther and in general by the liberal theologians of more recent times who are in that same tradition. This theory of weakness, as was shown above, is a complete misinterpretation of first-century Judaism. And it imposes on Paul a kind of introspective conscience that was not characteristic of him.

A second way to apply this interpretation is to stress the weakness of Christians in obeying the law of Christ. Particularly for persons coming from the Lutheran tradition, who are unable to take the argument of Chapter 6 with full seriousness, this interpretation leads to the conclusion that every Christian must recognize the impossibility of perfection.

The major problem with this theory of weakness is that it runs counter to the argument in Romans 6. Paul himself conveys no indication that he found it impossible to live out the Christian ethic. He exhorts his fellow Christians not to let *sin reign in your mortal bodies* (Romans 6:12).

In addition to going against the clear implications of Paul's argument in Romans, this interpretation also has some negative effects on the shaping of the Christian self-identity. It leads some people to a sense of self-pity and an expectation of failure. The constant exhortation to increase determination and willpower tends to drive competent people into a form of works-righteousness that is completely resistant to grace.

For those who succeed in fulfilling their Christian obligations, this interpretation leads them into an overly-boastful attitude concerning their superiority over others. A self-image that fluctuates between guilt feelings and superiority is one of the results of this misinterpretation of Romans 7.

A better interpretation is that Paul is depicting the dilemma of the self-righteous person in Romans 7. He is describing his own experience as a persecutor of the church, zealously convinced of the correctness of his own view and therefore encountering opposition against God. The dilemma of Romans 7 is explicitly laid out in Romans 10:1-4. Paul refers there to Jews who *have a zeal for God, but it is not enlightened.* Paul goes on to refer to resisting the *righteousness that comes from God,* and trying to establish their own righteousness instead of submitting to God's righteousness.

Romans 10:1-4 provides an accurate description of Paul's own situation before his conversion. It was not marked by a lack of zeal or a lack of righteousness, understood as conformity to the law. His basic flaw was his failure to recognize that God was revealed in a new and revolutionary way in Christ.

The failure to submit to the righteousness of God means that something profoundly wrong lay at the heart of the piety that had marked Paul's earlier life. Rather than weakness of will or the lure of his sensual desires, Paul's problem was his zealous commitment itself.

Only in the light of the cross event, as confirmed by the Resurrection, did Paul discover that his righteousness had a terrible internal flaw. The very good he sought to achieve, namely to obey God's will, turned against him, and he found himself an enemy of God.

This interpretation of Romans 7 helps to explain the religious and national zealotism in the current world. And it also allows us to understand the evidence within the Pauline letters in a straightforward way.

When Paul uses the term *flesh*, or *carnal*, he is talking about the unconsciously self-centered, self-justifying tendency of humans. The person who is *fleshly, sold under sin* is being held in bondage by this covetous orientation to the law. As long as the real motivation of the self is to gain justification to prove superiority over others, this element of unconscious sin has finally corrupted the goodness of the law. Thus when Paul refers to deliverance from *this body of death* in verse 24, he is describing the body dominated by the law of sin. The problem of humankind does not reside in our physical bodies. Rather, it is found in the sinful distortion of human desires that turn even the goodness of religion into its very opposite.

The Cure of Self-Righteousness (verse 25)

Verse 25 contains an allusion to the resolution of the

problem depicted in Romans 7. This line picks up the themes from 3:21–4:25 and 6:1-23. Paul is convinced that the grace of God as revealed in the Christ event finally exposed the self-righteousness of humans. In killing the Christ, the pious community was holding to its own righteousness. In zealously conforming to the law, religious persons found themselves opposing the righteousness of God.

But Paul also discovered in the Christ event the possibility of forgiveness. When a person is struck by grace, his or her former efforts to gain status through conformity to the law become unnecessary. The illusion that humans can produce the perfect good by themselves is replaced by the recognition of themselves as they really are. They are finite creatures whose best glory always falls short of the glory of God. But they are also creatures loved by God, unconditionally. A new basis for self-esteem is thus offered and a new kind of work begins to emerge. This new work is not aimed at boasting, but rather at responding to the boundless grace of God.

§ § § § § § §

The Message of Romans 7

The gospel provides a deliverance from the plight of self-defeating zealotism described in Romans 7. The gift of divine righteousness addresses the sense of vulnerability that provides the energy subverting the law. Paul shows, through this argument in Romans 7, that such behavior is a sign of returning to the old age of bondage to the law.

Any good achieved through such struggles for power will turn out to be evil. Only by understanding our lives as based solely on grace is there a possibility of overcoming the power of this attitude in which we oppose the status that others have because we want the status for ourselves and for our group alone. Thus when Paul says at the end of the chapter that *but with my flesh I serve the law of sin*, he is describing the actual motivational structure of the house churches in Rome, locked in their lethal battle with each other. Such battles are the flat repudiation of genuine faith. The same point could be made about similar battles in the modern world.

The hope for which Paul gives thanks in verse 25 is particularly relevant for persons and nations that discover contradictions between ideals and performance in their own history. Christ alone can deliver us from the past. His life and death reveal the essence of our dilemma. They convey to us an acceptance at so profound a level that we are able to accept ourselves as we are. Then we can cease the sinful striving to be the center of the world. This chapter is as relevant to individuals as it is to nations. Thanks be to God!

§ § § § § § §

Romans 8

Introduction to This Chapter

For many reasons, Chapter 8 is the indisputable high point of Romans. The emphasis on flesh versus spirit in verses 1-11 is one of the sources of the Wesleyan concept of holiness. Frequently, also, the idea of the *mind of the flesh* or *works of the flesh* has been connected with moral issues such as style of dress, forms of entertainment, and worldliness in general. While some of these trends are viewed by some Christians as problematic, the flesh and spirit dualism remains important.

Another important motif in Chapter 8 is the doctrine of the Spirit in verses 12-17 and 26-27. The Spirit conveys a sense of *sonship*, communicating unconditional acceptance that we are indeed children of God despite our faults. This idea is closely related to Wesley's Aldersgate conversion experience. The traditional Wesleyan emphasis on the work of the Holy Spirit in salvation and decision-making is sustained by this chapter.

Chapter 8 may be outlined as follows.

C. Providence and predestination (8:28-30)

III. Principalities and Powers (8:31-39)

Flesh and Spirit (8:1-17)

In this section, Paul deals with the cosmic struggle between flesh and spirit. The work of the spirit is integrated with the concept of salvation by portraying the spirit as it conveys unconditional acceptance, and therefore rightwising, to believers.

Liberation by Christ (8:1-4)

A key theme in Romans 8 is that we are *set . . . free from the law of sin and death* by Christ (verse 2). This theme dominates the entire section, and is developed in detail as Paul describes the work of Christ setting humans free from *sinful flesh*. By sending Christ in the flesh, Paul suggests that God *condemned sin in the flesh* (verse 3).

As we have seen from earlier chapters of Romans, Paul believes that the Christ event reveals the depth of human hostility against God. The function of Christ is to expose evil, but also to relieve humans from it. That is why Paul urges that the consequence of salvation is to walk *according to the Spirit* (verse 4).

This idea develops the key theme of Romans 6, that those who belong to the new age become *slaves of righteousness*. The means by which this transformation occurs, according to verse 3, is the sending of the Son in the *likeness of sinful flesh*. By this, Paul means that Christ was similar to us, yet not identical at the point of sharing the rebellion of humans, which is the essence of human sin. Christ shared our humanity but not our revolt. By exposing human self-righteousness and alienation, Christ set human beings free from their bondage.

The death of Christ is understood in Romans 8, as elsewhere in Romans, to be the exposure of human sin, its condemnation, and its overcoming by pure grace. His death results in a transformation of life, so that the law is actually accomplished. What God wills for humans, namely that they accomplish the good, is made possible when the human rebellion is ended. Grace overcomes the hostility that had distorted the human race, a point that links Romans 1:18-32 with the striking wording of Romans 8:7: *For the mind that is set on the flesh is hostile to God; it does not submit to God's law.*

The Contrast Between Flesh and Spirit (8:5-9)

In verses 5-9, Paul describes the two realms of the flesh and the Spirit in constant opposition to each other. Paul's use of the word *flesh* arose directly out of the Judaizer crises in the late 40s. *Flesh* came to designate the circumcised flesh of people who were advocating circumcision as necessary for salvation. The term also came to be identified by Paul as the cosmic power of the old age, the age of self-justification and sin.

This definition is what we find reflected in Romans 8. *Flesh* in Romans is characterized by the sinful desire to gain righteousness by works. Such a life leads to death because, in depending on our own flesh to gain righteousness, we come into conflict with the righteousness revealed in the new Son. The power of the flesh was broken by Christ, who came in the flesh. From that time on, life could be achieved through obedience to the law by means of the Spirit. In this way, the bondage to the flesh is superseded by life according to the Spirit.

In this chapter, Paul uses *Spirit* as the apportioned Spirit passed out to humans, as we can see in verse 15 as well as in verse 10. The Spirit is also identified with Christ. It is perceived to be the mark of the new age, manifesting itself in charismatic forms as well as in transformed ethical behavior. Therefore, the kind of dualism that Paul has in mind in Romans 8 is between the two ages, the age of Christ and the old age of Adam.

Paul's contention in this chapter is that these two ages are in opposition to each other. When Christians find themselves living according to the flesh, they are really falling back into the old age. Whether they intend it or not, the consequence is to come into opposition to God (verses 7-8).

The power sphere that attracts our loyalty determines our perspective (verse 5). When Paul describes this outlook in terms of hostility and resistance to the law of God, he has in mind his own previous experience, as we saw in Romans 7.

Paul's persecution of the church for not conforming to his own standards, and his resistance against Christ as a lawbreaker, was revealed to him on the Damascus Road as a sign of an unacknowledged hostility against God. Here in Chapter 8, Paul explains the kind of paralysis of the will that was described in 7:9: *The evil I do not want is what I do.* When Paul adds to this the idea that the mind of the flesh *does not submit to God's law*, he has in mind the aggressive misuse of the law as a means of status formation. It is not that Paul or other Jews of his time were unable to obey the law. Far from it. The problem, as Paul discovered in his own conversion, was that his perfect obedience to the law has unconsciously become a means of zealous rebellion against God.

Paul's point in this section is that the aggressive, competitive outlook of humans is determined by the old age. It is built into human institutions and cultural systems. That is why Paul believes that *flesh* is more than simply a human individual characteristic. It has to do with what we would call today "the social world." This kind of behavior pattern, the *mind of the flesh*, is pitted against a completely different outlook that Paul believes ought to be characteristic of the Christian community. The *mind of the Spirit* is capable of recognizing limitations. It is cooperative, and can therefore overcome hostility and class differences.

Paul's idea of two mindsets and two power spheres in combat with each other had a great relevance for the

Roman house church situation. In a sense, Paul is suggesting that the competition in Rome indicates that the mind of the flesh was still dominant there. What is needed in Rome are the features that Paul particularly identifies with the mind of the Spirit, *life and peace* (verse 6).

Life is understood to be an orientation toward realistic and mature relationships. It is full of thankfulness, but it is willing to accept death. Life in this sense is correlated later in the chapter with future hope and resilience in the face of opposition. The word *peace* in verse 6 has to do with overcoming barriers and hostility. It is a noncompetitive attitude. It involves harmony, not only with fellow humans, but also with the world around us. This was clearly a key issue for the Roman house churches. By contrast, the *mind of the flesh* is oriented, perhaps unconsciously, to competition and death. It is hostile, resulting in separation between humans and God as well as between humans themselves.

The Problem of the Body (8:10-11)

The word *bodies* is used in verses 10-11 in peculiar ways that need explanation. In light of Paul's reference to sacramental death and baptism in Romans 6:6, it is understandable that he could refer to the body as dead. What is puzzling in this context, however, is the addition of the phrase *because of sin*. This addition could lead to the mistaken conclusion that the power that destroyed the old self in baptism was sin itself. Paul probably inserted the word *sin* into the traditional description of baptism at this point in order to make clear that the reason the body must be put to death in baptism is because of sin, and not because of its material nature.

It is clear in these verses and elsewhere that Paul has a positive view of the body. His belief that the body will be enlivened is clear from the expression in verse 11 concerning Christ enlivening *your mortal bodies also through his Spirit which dwells in you*. This expression is strongly reminiscent of Romans 6:12, where Paul used the word *mortal* in order to correct the enthusiastic belief in the present possession of immortal existence.

A similar anti-enthusiastic focus here in verse 11 is apparent in the future form of the verb *enliven*, and in the double emphasis on the theme of Christ's resurrection from the dead. Thus the expression *mortal body* is probably used here, as in Romans 6, to prevent misunderstandings by gnostically inclined Christians.

Paul also refers to the body in verse 13 (see the commentary below).

Spirit and Sonship (8:12-17)

In verses 12-17, the function of the Spirit to convey a sense of acceptance and self-identity is stressed. Paul begins with another reference to the body in relation to death. He writes that *if by the Spirit you put to death the deeds of the body you will live. Body* is used here to provide an element of continuity between the old age and the new, between the old person and the new.

Paul often uses *body* as the characteristic term for the self. In this instance, what needs to be put to death is the self that performs deeds of pride and arrogance. Since a deed can only be *killed* by not performing it, this is an admonition to live and walk in the Spirit. Then we will leave behind the deeds that we, in our former lives under sin, were prone to perform.

The contrast between flesh and spirit manifests itself here, because *body* is used in a way that is virtually interchangeable with *flesh*. (See the discussion of *flesh* in the previous section on verses 10-11.)

That Christians are *led by the Spirit of God* (verse 14) was widely assumed in the Roman house churches. Paul connects this idea in a profound way to the main thesis of his letter, concerning the triumph of divine righteousness and the conveyance of unconditional acceptance. To be given the Spirit, according to verse 14, means to be confirmed as *sons of God*. This is elaborated in terms of the strong feeling of acceptance and belonging that is far from the *spirit of slavery* (see verse 15).

In verse 15, Paul goes on to connect the feeling of acceptance with a term that the early church picked up from the historical Jesus. In a unique way, Jesus referred to God as *Abba*, which in the original Aramaic language was the intimate address to God. The term might be translated *Pappa*, or *Daddy*. Since this was a foreign word for Paul's Greek audience, he translates it here with the term *Father*.

Jesus used this term for God to convey the intimate sense of acceptance that he felt. Thus, Paul suggests, when Christians find it possible to speak to God in this way, the Spirit is conveying to them that they are children of God.

It is interesting that Paul refers to our *crying out* of this acclamation. The ecstatic element of early Christian worship and devotional life is behind this statement, and it is quite likely that the term *Abba* was closely related to early Christian glossolalia (speaking in tongues). The inarticulate speech of early Christian ecstasy is being related here to the conveyance of unconditional acceptance. This means that the experience of the Spirit does not make Christians divine. Rather, when properly understood, it conveys to us that were are unconditionally loved by God. We are truly children of God, beloved and accepted.

That this experience of acceptance was open to females as well as males in the early church is conveyed when Paul moves from the language of *sonship* in verse 15 to the more inclusive term *children of God* in verses 16-17. As children, we are no longer outsiders. We are *heirs of God and fellow heirs with Christ*. We are no longer slaves and subordinates, but are honored members of the household of God and the inheritors of the promise.

Human Suffering (8:17-30)

This second major section deals with the hopeful suffering of the children of God. In these verses Paul discusses the cosmic context of the Christian faith.

Spirit, Suffering, and Hope (8:17-25)

At the end of verse 17 there is a phrase that announces the theme of the rest of Chapter 8: *provided we suffer with him in order that we may also be glorified with him.* In contrast to popular opinion concerning the gift of the Spirit and the impact of charismatic religious experience, Paul does not wish to allow the impression that it relieves people of the burden of finitude. Suffering remains a reality, even for those who have experienced the Spirit and have been transformed.

Paul goes on, in verses 18-25, to place suffering in a larger context. In the process, he places the work of the Spirit within the framework of world transformation. In these verses, the entire created order is depicted as yearning for the transformation of humans. Their sinful exploitation of the earth has caused the entire planet to be subject to decay and corruption (verses 20-21).

When humans are transformed, the earth itself will be restored as well. Responsibility for the soil will replace exploitation. Destruction of the forests and the waterways of the earth will be replaced by a transformation, as the entire world begins to reflect its intended glory with the rightwising of humans.

In the meantime, each Christian experiences the suffering and decay of the fallen order of things. The *groaning* of verses 22-23 is the passionate yearning for restoration. It is resistance against the distortion of the world order caused by sin. The final redemption of ourselves and of the world waits for the future promise that will be fulfilled only at the end of time (verse 23). This hope provides the realistic framework of Paul's doctrine of the Spirit.

Human Vulnerability and Weakness (8:26-27)

Most impressively, Paul understands the work of the Spirit as leading humans to accept themselves even in the midst of their vulnerability. That the Spirit *helps us in our weakness* (verse 26) is stressed in connection with early Christian prayer life.

Once again in these verses, Paul is interpreting the ecstatic prayer of the early church, marked as it was by speaking in tongues, prophecy, and various forms of excited and sometimes inarticulate utterance. When this occurs, Paul suggests, the Spirit is interceding with humans, making them know that they are accepted despite the suffering of the world and the inadequacies of their own abilities to express the truth.

The subconscious levels of the human mind and the emotive side of religious experience are here affirmed. But they are placed in the context of a suffering and groaning creation. In this sense, the Spirit conveys to us that even the least acceptable aspect of our selfhood, even our most inarticulate dimension, is accepted by God because God intercedes on our behalf through our weakness. The house churches in Rome desperately needed this resource in their struggles against adversity and in their conflict over the role of charismatic experience.

Providence and Predestination (8:28-30)

In verses 28-30, Paul affirms that even in the adverse experiences of life God works to achieve good with the chosen people. The old-fashioned translation of verse 28 is somewhat misleading: "Everything works together for good to those who love God." This translation often led to the false conclusion that God causes everything, including all evil, and that every evil event has a specific purpose in the divine plan. Paul is actually stating something much more limited and more reasonable. It is not that God causes all evil, but that in everything, whether good or bad, God works for good.

Paul had just affirmed in verses 18-25 that the creation had been subjected to futility because of human sin. Therefore it is clear that humans cause much of the evil in the world. This is also clear from the earlier argument of Romans. God acts as a providential force in all circumstances to create good out of evil.

The second half of verse 28 contains a clear reference to God's sovereignty in the form of the divine *purpose*. Paul is saying that God acts in the gospel to evoke faith, and that those who have experienced a transformation have a strong sense of having been elected by God. By referring to foreknowledge, predestination, calling, justifying, and glorifying, Paul stresses that humans are saved by God's intervention and not by their own actions.

In contrast to some doctrines of predestination, there is no hint here of what has been called "double predestination." Paul provides no explanation here for those who do not receive the gospel. And since he includes justification (rightwising) in this sequence, all the details of the previous argument concerning the inclusive scope of the gospel should be taken into account here. God remains impartial. And everyone is still potentially rightwised by grace as a gift.

Principalities and Powers (8:31-39)

These verses provide a conclusion not only for Chapter 8, but for all the material from 5:1 onward. The theme of these verses is that nothing can separate believers from the love of Christ.

Paul provides an elaborate list of the cosmic powers in verses 35-39. In the first century, people believed that the world was dominated by cosmic forces and powers. They personified the idea of evil and of social forces such as economics or government. They believed that there were powers in the heavens (*the heights*) and that there were powers below the surface of the earth (*the depth*). They were convinced that every human institution was something of an otherworldly power, capable of exercising an evil, superhuman control.

Human institutions and forces have an external structure, but they also have an internal spirit or ethos. We know this to be the case of the institutions for which we work and the governments that have been established by humans. Each has a different structure, and even those with similar structures have a different kind of spirit, shaped by the persons leading them and shaped by the peculiar history of the institution.

Paul's contention in verses 31-39 is that none of these institutions and forces is capable of separating humans from the love of Christ. Although the world remains fallen and these forces remain a reality, Christians have no need of losing heart. There is a basis for final confidence, a relational foundation for hope in the love of God that is demonstrated to us in that God *did not spare his own Son but gave him up for us all* (verse 32).

§ § § § § § §

The Message of Romans 8

The thrilling sequence at the end of Chapter 8 affirms not only the triumphant power of God over all human institutions, but also the basis of Christian realism and hope. These forces, which are often distorted and cause uncounted evil, and which contribute to the groaning of the whole creation, do not have ultimate power. They are in the process of transformation. And as Christians become agents of righteousness, their task is to work for the transformation of these forces and institutions.

The final transformation, of course, will not occur until the end of time. But in the meantime, Paul recommends an attitude that is the opposite of servility toward the principalities and powers of this world. Christians are not to be frightened of these powers, for they are incapable of separating believers from the love of God. Trusting in the power of the spirit over the flesh, and certain that their relationship with God is secure, contemporary Christians are called to take up this transformation of worldly institutions. If we took the gospel seriously, we too would face adversity with courage and become *more than conquerors through him who loved us* (verse 37).

§ § § § § § §

Romans 9–11

Introduction to These Chapters

In Romans 9–11 we encounter Paul's discussion of the problem of unbelieving Israel in relation to the triumph of divine righteousness. The key issue for Paul is stated in 9:6, whether the *word of God had failed*. If the gospel is indeed triumphant, as Paul has argued throughout Romans up to this point, then how does it happen that the first recipients of the gospel did not accept it? If the promise to Abraham was that through Israel all the Gentiles would be blessed, does the refusal of Israel to accept the gospel of Jesus Christ mean that God has taken back the promise? If God's word cannot be relied upon, then the gospel itself is untrue and the mission of Paul rests on a false foundation.

The issues of Jewish unbelief and world conversion are intimately linked in Paul's writings. This is an issue that he must answer in a satisfactory manner in order to make his gospel credible.

Romans 9–11 may be outlined as follows.

Following the Argument

Romans 9–11 has often been viewed as only loosely connected with the rest of Paul's letter to the Romans. Particularly to scholars oriented to the Lutheran tradition, who believed that the purpose of Romans was to teach the proper doctrine of justification by grace alone, the material in these chapters seemed quite problematic. Among traditional interpreters, only the Calvinists have taken great pleasure in the content of these chapters and have tried to make a case that they are connected closely with Romans.

In the approach we are following in this commentary, an integral relationship between these chapters and the rest of the argument of Romans is presupposed. The proofs that confirm the basic thesis of Romans 1:16-17 are being continued in 9:1–11:36. These three chapters are an extended discussion of the plight of Israel as it throws light on the central thesis concerning the righteousness of God.

The three chapters are divided into ten well-organized units. The first is the introduction (9:1-5), describing the tragic riddle of Israel's unbelief. Paul then opens the formal argument with 9:6-18, discussing the fate of Israel and the righteousness of divine election. In this section, Israel's destiny is seen to come through Isaac so that the true Israelites are *children of the promise* (see verse 8). The next section of the argument is 9:19-29, which answers an objection to Paul's argument. If Israel's destiny was the result of divine election, then how can God hold anybody else accountable for failing to perform? Paul deals with this by Scripture proofs concerning the potter and the clay and Israel's uneven relationship with God in the past.

In 9:30–10:4 Paul answers the question about the

righteousness of God by a doctrine of unenlightened zeal. Here he shows that Jewish zealotry had resulted in their rejecting the righteousness of God as it came to them in the Christ event. In the fifth section of the argument, 10:5-13, Paul argues that righteousness by faith alone is confirmed by Scripture. In this section he stresses the impartial quality of the righteousness of God, including Jews as well as Greeks.

In 10:14-21, Paul describes the gospel that was freely preached to the whole world but rejected by some of Israel. That this rejection was not unprecedented is proven by quotations about Israel's disobedience in the past. Then in 11:1-10, Paul provides an answer as to whether indeed God had rejected Israel. He contends that a remnant of Jews has indeed been responsive to the grace of God and that God had in no sense repudiated Israel.

In 11:11-24 Paul takes up the issue of the hidden purpose of Israel's rejection of the gospel. The gospel was then proclaimed to Gentiles so that the promise given to Israel that it would be a blessing to the Gentile world was fulfilled. The word of God has not been empty.

In the ninth section of the argument Paul lays out the mystery of Israel's salvation (11:25-32). After the appropriate number of Gentiles have been brought into the church, Paul believes that *all Israel will be saved*. The conclusion of the argument (11:33-36) is a doxology concerning the mysterious mind of God. This ends with a suitable reference to the all-inclusive power and scope of the divine rule and glory (11:36).

Introduction (9:1-5)

The opening lines of Romans 9 convey the deep sense of personal anguish that Paul had experienced at the repudiation by his fellow Jews of the gospel of Christ. The sincerity of his convictions on this point has apparently been called into question, because he refers to his *conscience* bearing witness to the truth of this anguish. Paul feels so strongly about this that he wishes that he himself were damned for the sake of his kinsmen, if they could only be included in the Christian fellowship (9:3).

Furthermore, that Paul cannot abandon a Jewish role in the Christian faith is elaborated by listing the eight privileges that belong to Israel. Here Paul picks up the theme left over from Romans 3:1-2. In answer to the question of what advantage the Jew has, he had written *much in every way*. But in Romans 3 Paul only dealt with one of these advantages, the fact that Israel had been entrusted with the oracles of God. Here he lays out all of the great contributions of Israel, contributions that were absolutely essential for a proper understanding of the gospel itself.

From this rather elaborate listing of Jewish prerogatives, it is clear that Paul does not wish to give any support to an anti-Semitic view of the faith, an issue which was apparently raging in Rome at the time of writing. The Jewish Christians were being discriminated against by the Gentile Christians. Paul is making a case here that by rejecting Jews, Gentiles were rejecting their own religious heritage. Every one of the eight attributes of the Jewish tradition had played a role in the earlier argument of Romans. Paul cannot conceive of a Christianity apart from Judaism.

Election and Israel's Fate (9:6-18)

The great religious heritage shared by the Jewish people would all be null and void if the faithfulness of God were jeopardized. This is the major issue that Paul wants to resolve in Romans 9–11. Does the repudiation of the gospel by a part of the Jewish people prove that God's word is not indeed powerful? We have traced this theme throughout Paul's letter, showing its relevance from the moment of its initial statement in the thesis of 1:16-17 that the gospel *is the power of God for salvation.* If the gospel is not powerful enough even to convince God's own people, what hope is there for the salvation of the world? And if God cannot prevail and make the promise stand, how can salvation be trusted? Thus, 9:6 states the fundamental issue to be dealt with in these three chapters, whether *the word of God had failed*.

After flatly denying that God's word failed, Paul supports his case on the premise that God's promise to Israel, given to Abraham, was that *through Isaac shall your descendants be named* (verse 7). This citation of an important principle of Jewish theology in Genesis 21:12 is interpreted in such a way that the true children of Isaac are understood to be *children of the promise*, persons who have responded to God's word.

Throughout Romans 9–11, Paul uses premises developed at the earlier argument of the letter. The issue that he faces in these chapters is so complex and serious that it has had to be postponed until these foundations were secure. Is it possible to believe that Israel was elected by God and yet that Israel had stumbled and was now being rejected? If the election of Israel had the power of God behind it, how could it be thwarted by human resistance?

Paul begins his formal argument in verse 7 by citing a text from Genesis which states that Israel's descendants will come through Isaac. The crucial interpretation of this text is offered in the next verse, using the categories developed earlier in Paul's letter. The *children of the flesh* are counterpoised here against the *children of the promise*.

This comparison allows Paul to reiterate the line first developed in Romans 4:13, that the true descendants of Isaac were persons who had responded to the promises of God. They were ones who received righteousness as a direct result of God's mercy, rather than of their own efforts under the law (9:11, 16). Paul is building a case here that those who rest their reliance on their *works* are not truly the children of Isaac. Only those who see their life resting entirely on the mercy and the call of God are the true children of Israel.

At this point, Paul is elaborating the theme of Romans 2:28-29, that the true Jew is the one who is circumcised in the heart. Similarly, Paul had argued in Romans 4:12 that Abraham was the father of those who *follow the example of the faith which our father Abraham had before he was circumcised.*

The point is that the word of God has not in fact failed; the true descendants of Isaac are being blessed.

The theme of election is essential for Paul's argument, as we can see in 9:11. Salvation does not come as a result of human initiative. It is not guaranteed to those who obey the law, because the law can so easily become a means of sustaining the claims of superiority.

Paul's reference to *works* in 9:11 evokes his earlier argument in Romans 3:20-28. Thus, Paul's radical doctrine of rightwising by grace alone is coordinated here with the doctrine of election. Since God will have mercy on whom God wills (9:18), recipients of salvation are called upon to recognize this election. The example of Pharaoh in 9:17-18 is used to substantiate the idea of salvation and damnation by divine election alone. Paul's major point here is that salvation is strictly due to divine mercy.

Individual Responsibility (9:19-29)

With his emphasis on divine election, Paul is able to take seriously the problem of stumbling. That humans had repeatedly rejected the call of God, and that Israel in particular had been unfaithful, is proven by the Scripture quotations in verses 25-29. In the last of these citations, verse 33, Paul correlates stumbling and the avoidance of stumbling with the possession of faith. Therefore, God's promise to be faithful to Israel has not been broken. Those who have faith and act as children of the promise remain under the power of God. To them God has remained faithful.

The Doctrine of Unenlightened Zeal (9:30–10:4)

Paul then goes on to explain this stumbling through a theory of unenlightened zeal which is closely related to his own conversion. Paul also dealt with this theme in Romans 7. Here in 10:3 he explicitly correlates the theme of righteousness with the rejection of Christ on the part of zealous Jews. In rejecting Christ, they were seeking to *establish their own, and did not submit to God's righteousness.*

The Book of Romans provides two elements that should determine the interpretation of the doctrine of election. (1) The inclusive argument of the rest of Romans shows that the gospel comes to all, that God's grace is unconditional, that God is no respecter of persons, and that God is the Lord both of the "weak" and the "strong." (2) The stress on human response to the gospel as determining one's fate is found in 10:8-17. There is no doubt that Pauline theology, therefore, offers a paradox that has tended to lead modern interpreters to take one side or other.

However, the paradox in Pauline theology is rooted in the experience of pure grace. Those who know themselves to be "children of the promise," recipients of a grace they could never deserve, recognize that their election and their own free response both stem from the same graceful root. When the doctrines of free will and divine election are developed beyond this starting point, they come into conflict with one another. But for Paul they derive from the same source.

That Paul was able to combine human responsibility with his view of election is evident in these verses. Here the ironic situation of Gentiles receiving righteousness and Jews losing it is discussed. Paul does not mention at this point his doctrine of election. There is no reference to divine wrath or displeasure, no hint that God has turned away from Israel. Instead Paul discusses the attitude of Jewish religionists toward righteousness. It is a righteousness by works.

Paul uses the promises developed in 3:21–4:25 when he discusses righteousness by works. He substantiates this by the citation from Isaiah 28:16 at the end of Chapter 9. The stone that the builders rejected, associated with *the stone that will make people stumble*, is a motif frequently used in early Christian confessions. Here the stumbling is linked to the motif of belief in Christ. The failure to respond to Christ in a timely manner is thus connected with the questions of faith and works: *He who believes in him* [God] *will not be put to shame* (9:33).

Paul's description of the unenlightened zeal of fellow Jews (10:2) is strongly reminiscent of his own former life as a Pharisee. *Zeal* is a term that Paul uses in describing his pre-Christian attributes in Philippians 3:6 and Galatians 1:14. Such zeal was characteristic of the fanatical, revolutionary piety and violence of first-century Judaism.

Such zeal determined the moral convictions of individual believers and identified those convictions flatly with the divine will. Phinehas was a model at this point because in the lynching murder that he committed, the tradition affirmed that his zeal was the *zeal of the* LORD (Numbers 25:11).

Paul sees the *righteousness of God* manifest in the Christ event. He interprets his own earlier life and the current situation of unbelieving Jews as expressing the kind of hostility against Jesus as a lawbreaker that had contributed to his death. Christ as the revelation of the righteousness of God became a stumbling block, because he revealed the hostility of zealots. A false form of righteousness is here counterpoised against the righteousness manifest in the Christ event, a righteousness that involved unconditional acceptance of outsiders, and mercy rather than violence against those who sinned.

Paul sees the Christ event as revealing the fundamental flaw of zealous religion. And he sees that same zealous religion at the heart of the Jewish rejection of the gospel in his own time. The dilemma that we saw in Romans 7:7-25 comes here to its final expression: The very persons most passionately devoted to achieving the will of God ended up opposing it.

The underlying issue in the rejection by zealous Jews of the revelation of the righteousness of God in Christ was the law (see verse 4). The fact that Jesus was a lawbreaker, and that he was executed in a way that revealed to popular perception that he was a lawless sinner, made the center of the gospel an issue of disrepute among loyal Jews. The statement about the relation between Christ and the law in 10:4, however, is rather complicated and requires some sorting out.

Several recent studies of Romans 10:4 have lent weight to the alternative that Paul intended to say that Christ is the goal of the law. A thorough investigation of the Greek word behind this translation suggests that originally it meant an apex, an aim, or a completion. In philosophical discussions during Paul's time, this term was frequently used in a technical sense to depict a final cause, goal, or purpose.

The verbal form of the term used here in verse 4 is found in Romans 2:27, which everyone agrees should be translated as *fulfill or complete the law*. Thus the idea of goal or fulfillment is characteristic of Paul's use of this group of terms.

The consequence of this recent research is that Romans 10:4 provides a much less polemical basis than was previously thought for the relation between Jews and Christians. Paul's argument in this section is that the ultimate purpose of the law was that all persons, Jews and Gentiles alike, might find righteousness. If Christ is the goal of the law, the path of faith can be pursued without repudiating the Torah.

A crucial point here is that there is no need to become anti-Semitic to be a Christian. There is no need for Jews, if they become Christians, to repudiate their legacy of the Torah. That Paul believes this is clearly indicated by his statement of the eight advantages the Jews have in 9:4-5. It is also strongly confirmed by the formulation Paul used to conclude Romans 3:31: *On the contrary, we uphold the law.* This verse has always given exegetes a difficult time because it seems to flatly contradict what Paul wrote in Romans 10:4. But when Romans 10:4 is understood to say that Christ is the goal of the law, the contradiction obviously disappears.

Righteousness by Faith Alone (10:5-13)

In these verses, Paul depicts the gospel as available to all persons, capable of saving all persons. Its availability is stressed by the idea of its nearness (see 10:8); no person in the Roman churches or synagogues was too distant to hear it. The very words of Scripture that they cited in their prayers and liturgies (10:8) affirmed the grace of God that was the essence of the gospel. The only thing keeping anyone from salvation was rejecting this good news (10:9-10).

But the content of Paul's gospel, as described in earlier parts of Romans and even in this chapter, needs to be kept in mind. What Paul has in view here in the *word* and the *word of faith* is not a new ideology. It is not a set of dogmas that people have to swallow. It is rather the revelation in the life and death of Jesus of the perverted zeal of religious fanaticism, of the universal tendency toward rebellion and self-destruction that marks all people everywhere.

The good news in this *word of faith* is that in Christ human rebellion was met by unconditional grace and forgiveness. This gospel strikes to the heart of human vulnerability and fear, the sources of sinful rebellion. And by accepting this message, humans can be *saved* (10:10). They can be saved from themselves, saved from the natural consequences of a sinful life, and also saved from the wrath to come. As Paul had argued earlier in Romans, continuing the life under the curse of Adam, shaped by self-will and fleshly arrogance, is a life leading toward death. Only righteousness has the promise of life within it.

In this section Paul stresses the universality of salvation. In 10:11 he cites Isaiah 28:16 to the effect that *no one who believes in him will be put to shame.* This emphasis is picked up in succeeding verses that are reminiscent of the earlier argument of Romans. Both Greeks and Jews are offered this gospel. God is impartial; there is no discrimination on the basis of race or background. The Lord bestows riches *upon all who call upon him* (10:12).

The Rejection of the Gospel (10:14-21)

Given the unifying power of the word, it is fitting to celebrate the beauty of preaching this gospel (see verses 14-15). But Paul reiterates the key role of human responsibility in verse 16. Salvation in this context is not construed as a result of divine arbitrary judgments, but rather as a result of human willing response or rejection. The passage then concludes with the great formula widely used in Protestant preaching. *Faith comes from what is heard, and what is heard comes by the preaching of Christ* (verse 17).

The source of world transformation and of the salvation of all people everywhere is the proclamation of this good news. When it evokes faith, salvation becomes a reality. This argument thus provides crucial support for Paul's purpose of world mission in Romans.

God Did Not Reject Israel (11:1-10)

In Romans 11, Paul deals directly with the issue of Jewish rejection of the gospel. God does not respond to this by rejecting Israel (11:1), because a faithful remnant has been saved by grace (11:5).

Why Israel Rejected the Gospel (11:11-24)

But even those who have rejected the gospel are not without purpose and hope, as Paul sees it. Because of the repudiation of the gospel of Christ by some Jews, the gospel was preached to the Gentiles. God was able to use even unbelief for the purpose of the larger mission.

Paul has in mind here perhaps the historical reality of the earliest Christian mission, which came about somewhat inadvertently, according to the Book of Acts. After the Jewish zealots had killed the first Christian martyr, Stephen, the church was scattered and the gospel was thereby spread to the Gentile world (Acts 8:1-4).

In verses 17-24 Paul deals with the feelings of superiority on the part of Gentiles who had received the gospel, in contrast to some Jews who had repudiated it. Paul's wording in this passage seems clearly to reflect an anti-Semitic feeling on the part of Gentile Christians in Rome. Their house church experience as well as their salvation was embodied in the arrogant boast that Paul constructs in verse 19: *Branches were broken off so that I might be grafted in.* In fact, the Gentiles had received the gospel only after some Jews had repudiated it and had begun persecuting the followers of Jesus.

Furthermore, in the Roman situation the Gentile house churches had flourished only after the synagogues had closed under the edict of Claudius. Yet Paul is unwilling to allow this arrogance to stand. He issues the warning in verse 22 against presuming on the *kindness . . . of God* and falling under judgment. The background for this warning is the earlier argument of Romans that shows the disastrous consequence of human pride.

The Mystery of Israel's Salvation (11:25-32)

However, the ultimate purpose of God is yet to be achieved, Paul contends. Israel's zeal for salvation will be provoked by the saving of the Gentiles so that ultimately *all Israel will be saved* (11:11, 25-26).

The scope of salvation and of the Christian mission is to be universal. Otherwise, the word of God would indeed have failed. In light of these considerations, there is no reason for Gentile arrogance and discrimination to be aroused by the current repudiation of the gospel by zealous Jews, as Paul sees it.

Conclusion (11:33-36)

Chapter 11 closes with the remarkable juxtaposition between the *mystery* of the final conversion of the Jews (verse 25) and the inscrutable will and knowledge and mind of God (verses 33-36). Paul is true at this point to his convictions that the first and second commandments must be obeyed.

§ § § § § § §

The Message of Romans 9–11

No human theology, even Paul's own, can finally penetrate the "mind of God." There is a need for humility both in the church and in Paul's mission. Yet to this one transcendent God belong all things and persons because they derive ultimately from the same God (see 11:36).

God is glorified when zeal is transformed by the gospel and when the world is thereby reunited. Paul is concerned not only with Jewish zeal, but with Gentile zeal as well. All people in Paul's time as well as our own belong together under the one true and transcendent God, and Paul's confident hope is that they shall one day discover this destiny—together.

§ § § § § § §

Romans 12

Introduction to This Chapter

As we move from the theological to the ethical argument of Romans, there is a need to counter the tendency to see this material as secondary or even as unrelated to the earlier portions of the letter. If the theme of the entire letter is the righteousness of God, the material from 12:1 through 15:13 deals with the practical requirements of righteous living.

Since many of the admonitions in these chapters are traditional, reflecting the shared ethical heritage of Judaism and early Christianity, there is also a tendency to approach them as a rather disorganized list of exhortations. In fact, the material in these chapters is tightly structured with Chapter 12 providing the foundation for all the rest.

Chapter 12 may be outlined as follows.

I. The Theme of the Section (12:1-2)
II. The Use of Christian Gifts (12:3-8)
III. The Struggle Between Good and Evil (12:9-21)
    A. Guidelines for genuine love (12:9)
    B. Life in the congregation (12:10-13)
    C. Life outside the congregation (12:14-20)
    D. Conclusion (12:21)

The Theme of the Section (12:1-2)

Verses 1-2 provide the earliest systematic basis for a Christian ethic. The motivation for good behavior developed in these two verses is derived from the entire first eleven chapters of Romans, as summarized by the expression, *the mercies of God.*

Paul opens his ethical section of Romans with an appeal to respond appropriately to the experience of grace. The motivation for good behavior is not the earning of status or gaining of advantages for oneself, but is responding to God's mercy toward sinners such as us. The entire earlier argument of Romans concerning salvation by grace alone should be recalled by this expression. The gratitude we feel for receiving God's love is therefore what impels us toward ethical actions.

Just as ancient Israelites responded to God's intervention in their behalf by offering sacrifices on the altar, so Christians are to express their sense of gratitude by giving their bodies as a *living sacrifice* in their everyday actions. Since Paul uses the term *body* to refer to the whole person, he means that our daily work and leisure, our family obligations and community activities, our intimate as well as our social relations are all to be done in praise of God.

The *spiritual worship* required of Christians is paradoxically a matter of our bodies. In this way Paul has overcome the traditional split between the spiritual and the physical realms. The focal center of Christian worship is not the religious sanctuary but everyday life. This letter, which was undoubtedly being read in the Roman house churches, thus directs attention beyond the joyous celebration of believers toward the arena of the outside world.

The problem of a proper relation to this outside world surfaces in verse 2. The typical pattern for ethical instruction is conformity. Education during Paul's time as well as our own requires children to learn traditional values and to conform to standard rules of behavior. Both as children and as adults, we conform to the expectations of others in order to gain approval. This is the opposite motivation from what Paul desires.

Paul urges his listeners not to behave in certain ways to earn the love of others and of God. Rather, according to Paul, the essence of the Christian faith is that we have already been given such love without earning it, and thus are free to respond in gratitude.

In earlier chapters of Romans, Paul showed that Christians are set free from the law of public approval. To continue in conformity, therefore, would entail falling back under the law, which leads to futility and death. Rather than being *conformed to this world*, Paul calls us to allow the gospel to *transform* the way we think as well as the reasons we act. The ongoing process of being changed by the gospel aims at the discernment of *the will of God* (verse 2).

Paul assumes that what God wants of us must continually be ascertained, that we cannot finally rely on rules or human authorities to tell us what to do. That would involve reverting back to obeying the law, refusing the new relationship in which the Spirit of God speaks in our hearts (see 8:9-17). The new ethic of living sacrifice responds directly to God, constantly communicating through prayer and praise. Out of this communion, what God wants us to do can be perceived and accomplished.

Paul's admonition about proving the will of God is directed to "you all," so to speak. The combined intelligence and experience of a Christian community is required to break free from conformity and to discern freshly what God wants us to do here and now. The abiding standards of holy behavior, *the good and acceptable and perfect*, require updating and application in constantly changing circumstances. The church should never forget that it lives in a fallen creation by hope rather than by sight (see 8:18-27).

In proving and testing out what God wills, we must constantly remind ourselves that *our knowledge is imperfect and our prophecy is imperfect* (1 Corinthians 13:9). Yet we are called as children of a loving Father (see Romans 8:15) to respond in gratitude, by acting in accordance with the knowledge and prophecy our communities of faith have been granted. The lamp for our feet may be flickering but it suffices for the next step.

The Use of Christian Gifts (12:3-8)

In verses 3-8 Paul turns to the question of the spiritual and moral resources of the church. First he counters the danger of overrating those resources (verse 3); then he turns to the opposite danger of underrating them (12:4-6a). Since this is a sensitive task, he refers to the authority with which he had founded and counseled early Christian congregations. *The grace given to me* alludes to Paul's calling as an apostle to the Gentiles (see Romans 1:5 and 15:15-16, as well as 1 Corinthians 3:10 and Galatians 2:9).

The contrast in 12:3 that would have been readily understood in Rome is disguised by modern translations. A literal translation of this important sentence is: For by the grace given to me I enjoin every one among you not to be superminded above what one ought to be minded, but to set your mind on being soberminded, each according to the measuring rod of faith that God has dealt out. To be "superminded" is contrasted here with "soberminded," the one involving a proper sense of one's limits and the other falling prey to the prideful impression of being superior to others. When Christians believe they are superior, they lose sight of the fact that they are saved only by grace.

Paul develops in verse 3 a unique idea of an individualized *measure of faith*, understood as a kind of measuring device by which ethical and theological judgments can be reached. The Greek word for measure, *metrono*, which is related to the modern words *metronome* and *meter*, usually signifies a means of measurement. Each Christian is given a unique experience of faith, evoked as the Spirit makes the gospel of divine love relevant to the condition of the heart.

This measuring rod of faith must be retained by each Christian as the basis of a proper relationship with God and the world. But if we become "superminded" about our measuring rod, the typical result is to coerce others to accept our theology and ethical judgments.

Paul is probably dealing here with a widely shared problem in the early church. The conflicts in the Roman house churches appear to have been related to such arrogance, overlooking the fact that God has called persons of other racial and economic backgrounds whose measuring rods are somewhat different. The conflicts between the so called "weak" and "strong" in 14:1–15:7 are clear evidence that Paul's admonition on this point was necessary. Christians revert to the domination and partisanship of the pagan world when they begin to regard themselves as superhuman; Paul regards this as being dangerously *conformed to this world* (verse 2).

The variety and intrinsic worth of individual congregational members are affirmed in verses 4-8. This affirmation counters the tendency of these members to feel inferior about their gifts.

The *charismata,* or *gifts,* of individual members are to be perceived as expressions of divine grace (verse 6). Therefore, any attempt to rank these gifts in value is out of order. Paul avoids the numerical ranking system he employs in 1 Corinthians 12:28. Also, he does not specifically mention prestigious offices such as apostles.

Each gift is to be exercised in accordance with the intrinsic standards of that gift: Serving requires a different talent from exhortation, and administering aid demands a different attitude from the consoling work of mercy. The guideline for prophecy is more precisely described as *in proportion* or *according to the standard of faith,* which is related to the measuring rod of faith given to each Christian, according to 12:3.

But the main exhortation in this section is *let us use them* (verse 6). Paul wishes to counter the tendency to allow the unique gifts of each congregational member to lie fallow while prestigious leaders take over the church. He advocates the radically egalitarian principle that we are *individually members one of another* (verse 5). Whether slave or free, rich or poor, male or female, Greek, Roman or Jew, each member's service is essential if the will of God is to be followed.

An ethic that takes its start from the generous mercy of God cannot allow the human distinctions of the secular world to hold sway in the Christian community.

Guidelines for Genuine Love (12:9)

The opening command in the final section of the chapter (verses 9-21) deals with the primary ethical standard for the church, *love*. Generous, self-giving love, *agape*, is the human response to the love and mercy of God conveyed by Christ to each person (see Romans 5:5).

Paul does not command Christians to love; he seems to take it for granted. If we have been transformed by unearned love, passing such love on to others is the natural instinct of Christians. Paul concentrates instead on the issue of genuineness. It is likely that Paul had already encountered false forms of love that are listed here: sentimental love that is strong on feeling but short on help; manipulative love that masks the desire to dominate others; soft love that refuses the demands of personal and community integrity.

By linking love with the passionate emotions of hating evil and cleaving to good, Paul keeps alive the theme of moral discrimination that he had stated in 12:2. This means that *agape* is tough love; it means being willing to struggle for what is right even if we cannot always agree on what that entails. The discrimination between good and evil is never finished; it requires the input of each member of the community of faith.

Life in the Congregation (12:10-13)

The first ten admonitions that follow the command about genuine love deal with the community of faith, whose health and vitality are essential if love is to survive. It is useless to speak of love in the abstract. Love has to be embodied in real communities of potentially awkward neighbors and sometimes abrasive church members.

Brotherly love, *philadelphia*, is to be sustained with *affection* which must be mutual (verse 10a). *Outdo one another* (12:10b) is a contrived translation that conveys an inappropriate element of competition. Paul probably meant "taking the lead in honoring one another," which involves generous treatment of outsiders—a serious problem in Rome (see 14:1–15:7).

The next two verses (verses 11-12) deal with keeping the spiritual springs of love flowing through religious enthusiasm, sincere devotion, and prayerful constancy in adverse circumstances.

Verse 13 then turns to the practical expression of love in practicing hospitality and assisting needy *saints*. Both are critical issues in the Roman congregation when refugees from the edict of Claudius are currently returning to their abandoned homes and businesses.

Life Outside the Congregation (12:14-20)

An important issue for returning refugees is dealt with in verses 14-20: the tendency to resent those who have persecuted them and to seek vengeance for wrongs. Since giving way to such natural feelings would betray the new life in the Spirit inaugurated by the love of Christ, Paul suggests that the transformation (verse 2) could take the form of blessing persecutors (verse 14), refusing to repay evil for evil (verse 17), living at peace with hostile enemies (verse 18), and leaving vengeance up to God (verses 19-20). These are crucial guidelines for genuine love, but the capacity to carry them out is anything but natural for persons who have been abused and exiled as many of the Roman Christians had been.

At this point it is important to recall the argument of the earlier chapters of Romans, which laid the foundation to make such love possible. Only those who have experienced God's love, conveyed to the inner depths of the heart by the Spirit (5:5), have the resources to pass love on to others in so generous a manner. Only those whose arrogance has been broken (2:17–3:20) and whose hope is entirely anchored on God rather than on human possibilities (4:1-25) are free to live in harmony with others (12:15-16). Only those who have been set free from the laws of conformity and competition (7:1-25) are capable of associating with the lowly without conveying a feeling of conceit (12:16).

To understand the background of Paul's discussion of vengeance in verses 19-20, we must realize that large segments of the Jewish community in the period prior to the Jewish-Roman war of A.D. 66-70 favored a vigilante strategy. Modeling their behavior on the heroic tales in the Old Testament, they believed that vengeance against evildoers would achieve divine ends. In particular, these advocates of Jewish vigilance felt that the Roman governing authorities should be opposed on principle, and with force. And it was natural in this environment that many persons who had suffered injustices felt themselves called by the heroic stories to take the law into their own hands, to avenge themselves and thus to redeem Israel.

In view of the popularity of personal vengeance in the ancient world, the admonition to *leave it to the wrath of God* (verse 19) involves refusing to *be conformed to this world* (12:2). Paul reaffirms at this point a cardinal principle of ancient and modern jurisprudence, that no one should try to judge his or her own cause. Vengeance is to be left to other agencies. The *wrath of God* referred to in 12:19 takes the form of governmental law enforcement (see 13:1-5) as well as the expectation of the final judgment.

The responsibility of individual Christians is spelled out in verse 20, where Paul cites Proverbs 25:21-22 concerning caring for the enemy. The *burning coals* on the head aim at evoking remorse and repentance on the part of persecutors, an essential aim of love. It is important to observe, however, that Paul does not promise automatic happy endings for those who love their enemies. As the earlier chapters of Romans have made clear (see 5:3-5; 8:18-25), Christians must live in hope because the old age of hostility and violence is still present.

§ § § § § § §

The Message of Romans 12

This chapter provides a coherent basis for a realistic ethic in the modern world. It calls for an ongoing transformation, not only of moral standards but also of the world itself. But evil is taken as seriously here as it is in Chapter 8, providing a realistic context for the ethic of sacrificial love.

Living sacrifices (12:1) will continue to be required in the ongoing and still unfinished effort to *overcome evil with good* (12:21).

§ § § § § § §

Romans 13:1–15:13

Introduction to These Chapters

In these chapters Paul takes up some of the most difficult issues as far as the situation in Rome was concerned. The question of how to relate to the Roman authorities was very touchy and had played a role in the expulsion of Christian leaders during the time of the edict of Claudius. The question of the relation between love and law divided the conservatives from the liberals. The question of how to respond to the anticipated return of Christ and what kind of ethic was required in the end-time period was complex and difficult. Finally the issues of mutual tolerance between groups in the house churches were highly sensitive. Paul leaves these issues until the latter part of Romans because now there is a sufficient basis to create a compelling argument.

This section may be outlined as follows.

I. Christians and Government (13:1-7)
II. Love and the End Times (13:8-10)
III. Moral Alertness in the Final Days (13:11-14)
IV. Guidelines for the Weak and Strong (14:1-23)
V. Accepting Outsiders (15:1-6)
VI. Summary Statements (15:7-13)

Following the Argument

The material in 13:1–15:13 fits into the final exhortative section of Romans. It provides guidelines for living in righteousness in relation to the problems faced by the

Roman house churches.

The structure of the material is fairly easy to follow. Verses 1-7 deal with the issue of proper subjection to the government. Verses 8-10 set forth the relation of love to law. Verses 11-14 describe and call for moral alertness in the final days. Verses 1-23 in Chapter 14 provide guidelines for the weak and the strong and for mutual upbuilding in the congregation. Verses 1-6 in Chapter 15 provide an exhortation to follow Christ's example in accepting outsiders into the church. Finally, 15:7-13 draws the preceding argument together and provides the motivation for world mission and unification, the ultimate goals of the letter.

Christians and Government (13:1-7)

This is one of the most controversial passages in Romans. Somewhat in contrast with his skeptical statements about the ruling authorities in earlier letters, Paul affirms here that government derives ultimately from God and that the Christians in Rome should respond to governmental decrees as if divine authority were behind them.

This rationale for government has caused a great deal of controversy in Christian history. Persons who take this section literally become conservative in their attitude toward the state and find it difficult to express opposition even when the state becomes thoroughly evil. It is important therefore to read 13:1-7 in the light of the premises laid down in 12:2.

Paul does not abandon the need for discrimination. And despite the sweeping wording of verses 1-7, Paul does not wish the Christian community simply to conform itself to the whims of the Roman Empire. Romans 13:3-4 reminds Christians of the ultimate purpose of governmental power: to achieve the good. When this goal is coordinated with the appeal to conscience in verse 5, there are resources at hand to carry out the kind of discriminating ethical action called for at the beginning of Chapter 12.

Apparently there were local circumstances that led Paul to this sweepingly positive rationale for governmental authority. The community had been shaken by revolutionary sentiments, particularly during the time prior to the edict of Claudius in A.D. 49. At that time, zealous Jewish opponents of the early Christian mission probably were influenced to some degree by the revolutionary movements in Israel and elsewhere. It seems unlikely that Christians were directly involved in this revolutionary activity, but they were certainly influenced and their fate was shaped by it. In particular, those who suffered the exile from Rome had come face to face with the price of revolutionary activity.

More to the point, for the Roman audience, was the struggle over tax resistance which marked this period of Roman administration. A controversy over excessive taxes was rumbling during this time, and Paul uses the precise bureaucratic categories for the two taxes in question, translated as *taxes* and *revenue* in 13:7. This latter tax was a form of customs duties. It seems quite likely that Paul is encouraging the church not to get involved in this agitation over the legitimacy of taxes. This would have been a particularly sensitive point in the two house churches (see Part Thirteen) that were involved in governmental service, perhaps even in tax collection.

A final consideration is that Paul wrote these lines during a period of exemplary law enforcement in the early years of the Nero administration. When Nero began to drift into lawlessness in A.D. 62, the government began to play a very different role. The subsequent persecution of Christians and the widespread lawlessness of governmental officials that erupted periodically were certainly not in view when Paul wrote these lines. It is therefore wise for the Christian community to view 13:1-7 as general guidelines whose applicability needs to be assessed at each point by collective wisdom. The premises laid down in Romans 12:2 must be particularly kept in mind in the interpretation of this section.

Love and the End Times (13:8-10)

In these verses Paul takes up the delicate task of synthesizing the love ethic that would have been favored by the "strong" in Rome and the respect for the law which would have marked the ethic of the "weak" in Rome.

Paul argues in these verses that love fulfills the law and that those who obey the law do so out of love. Those who love follow the guidelines of the law. The continuing usefulness of the law as guidelines for Christian ethics is affirmed here, but the legalistic motivation is eliminated. In this sense, Paul probably takes part from the "weak" and part from the "strong."

Any form of abject submission to the law is eliminated here, consistent with the premises laid down in Romans 12:2. Persons set free from the law need to continue to respect the law as providing basic guidelines for ethical decision making. The law in this sense provides guidelines for understanding *what is good and acceptable and perfect* (Romans 12:2). This is the goal for which all day-to-day Christian decision making should strive.

Moral Alertness in the Final Days (13:11-14)

The horizon for Christian decision making is the impending end of time, as far as Pauline theology was concerned. There is no doubt from the wording in this section that Paul expected the end of history very soon. But rather than advocating the relaxation of ethical urgency, Paul uses the fact that *the night is far gone* to argue for an intensified sensitivity about the distinction between behavior appropriate for the old age and for the new.

In verses 13-14, Paul names some of the *works of*

darkness that were particularly popular in Rome. The first pair of works of darkness conveys a life pattern of self-destruction. The term translated as *reveling* originally was used to depict the festal procession in honor of the god Dionysus. It connotes irresponsible carousing, with loss of self-control and drunkenness.

This kind of escapist behavior was a possible response to the fact that the end of time was rapidly approaching. But Paul believes that such behavior is intrinsically destructive and a sign of reversion to the old age.

The second pair of works of darkness that Paul names is *debauchery and licentiousness*. The first term is literally *beddings*, which implies the willingness to have sexual intercourse with anyone who is available. The second term is closer to what we would now call sensualities. It connotes behavior that experiments with sensations, lacking internal moral standards that might set any limits.

In the Rome of the first century, such exploitative actions were generally viewed as harmless. Paul identifies them as *works of darkness* to be avoided by members of the new age.

The final pair of works of darkness that Paul lists is more straightforward in its translation: *quarreling and jealousy*. We might identify these as related to the desire to dominate other people. Quarreling is typical of those who desire to dominate others, while jealousy is the response of those who wish to dominate but fail to do so. At the root of both is the yearning to be ahead of others and to rule over others.

In the highly competitive society of the Greco-Roman world, where the class structure was particularly oppressive, these traits were widely expressed and generally accepted. Studies of the psychology of the Greco-Roman world indicate that the sense of self-identity was substantially dependent on admiration by others. This produced a highly competitive social environment in which domination was simply assumed. Paul contends, however, that domination is inappropriate for people who have experienced unconditional grace. The self-identity of the members of the new age no longer requires public acceptance and popularity.

Paul's effort in verses 11-14 was to sensitize Christians to make sure that their behavior was consistent with the time in which they lived. Escapism, exploitation, and domination were inappropriate despite their popularity in the society in which the Roman house churches found themselves.

Paul's alternative was to *put on the armor of light, to put on the Lord Jesus Christ* (13:12, 14). The armor metaphor implies a realism about the dangers of the works of darkness and the need to defend against them. The righteous relationships in which the blessing of God can prosper are to replace the *works of the flesh* (13:14). The self-centered behavior that marked the time before Christ is not to be reaffirmed now that the final age is dawning.

Guidelines for the Weak and Strong (14:1-23)

In these verses Paul counters the expression of the selfishness of the old age within the house churches at Rome. The fundamental thrust of his argument is that to despise and judge one another is to lose sight of who the Lord is. If God has *welcomed* my opponent (14:3), and if God is the one before whom my opponent *stands or falls*, and if my opponent *will be upheld, for the Master is able to make him stand* (14:4), then the expression of the competitive spirit constitutes competition with God. The definition of sin as suppression of the truth about the distinction between the creature and the Creator (see 1:18-32) is here applied to the situation of conflict within the congregation.

Verses 5-9 emphasize the lordship of Christ. There are no less than nine references to the fact that each side in the controversy carries out its ethical actions and liturgical programs in honor of God. To call our competitors' actions fundamentally into question, therefore, is to disturb this relationship. In the final analysis it is to declare war on the Lord, to violate the first commandment.

The final appeal to respect the relation that other persons have to the Lord is in verses 10-12, where Paul refers to the prospect of the final judgment. Once again the urgent end-time circumstance of 13:11-14 is used to motivate ethical behavior. When we face the final judgment, the question of submission to the Lord alone will be asked. None of us will be asked at that point whether our brothers and sisters have been responsible. Each *shall give account* of his or her activities to God (14:12).

Accepting Outsiders (15:1-6)

The judgmental spirit that was dividing the church constituted, in effect, a refusal to bow the knee to God. It was an effort to replace that final judgment with our own judgment. Here a form of the eschatological reservation is being used for the sake of mutual tolerance in the church.

Summary Statements (15:7-13)

In 15:7 Paul provides a summary statement concerning the tolerant, mutual acceptance that he has argued for in the last two chapters. At the same time, he draws together themes that unify the entire letter.

The first clause in verse 7, *welcome one another, therefore*, summarizes the tolerant perspective of the last two chapters. The term *tolerance* is somewhat misleading here, of course, because our modern sense of the term is grudging acceptance. Paul is asking for the active welcome of one's competitors. What is at stake here is accepting the basic legitimacy of the other side. Since the competitors worship the same God and are beloved by the same God that the Romans worship, it is inappropriate to treat them as outsiders.

The second clause of verse 7 provides the rationale for this mutual welcome: *as Christ has welcomed you.* This statement reiterates the theme of 14:3-4. But it also draws together the theological argument of the entire early section of Romans. The idea that Christ welcomes sinners unconditionally was laid out in 3:21-31.

That God welcomes sinners who have made themselves enemies of God was powerfully stated in Romans 5:8-10. What is particularly striking about this rationale for tolerance is the full integration with faith. Often tolerance in a practical sense rests merely on the sense that final truth is unavailable. In this instance Paul urges a kind of active tolerance which is based on the fact that Christ has been tolerant to us. The same kind of vigorous welcome that marks Christ's dying for others is to be expressed in the welcome that the Christian communities in Rome pass on to one another.

The final purpose of mutual welcome is stated in the words *for the glory of God.* The true glory of God manifests itself in the overcoming of self-centered competition. Whereas the desire to defeat our enemies and to be victorious over our church competitors provides glory to ourselves, Paul urges a strategy that gives recognition of the variety of God's creation.

Acknowledging God's unconditional acceptance of our enemies gives glory to God rather than to us. By placing that mutual welcome under the power of Christ's welcome, Paul completes the theme of the righteousness of God. As we have seen, God's righteousness is manifest only when God's glory is triumphant. If this glory can manifest itself in the church, then a vital new sense of mission will emerge and the Roman house churches will take up the task of world unification. They will engage in mission not to prove their superiority over others, but rather to share the welcome which they had already themselves experienced in Christ.

In verses 5-6 and verse 13, Paul draws together the

argument with benedictions that synthesize his desires for the congregation and express the burden of his previous argument. The first benediction summarizes principally the material from Romans 14:1–15:5. The second draws together the argument of the entire epistle. The term translated *believing* in 15:13 is the familiar word *faith*, which relates to the thesis of Romans in 1:16-17.

§ § § § § § §

The Message of Romans 13:1–15:13

The hope lifted up in this section is for the unification of the world through the gospel. This hope is as relevant for the twentieth century as it was for the first century.

The centrality of the Gentile mission for the entire letter of Romans is magnificently caught by the series of Scripture quotations that lead up to this final benediction (15:9-12). The hope is that when the gospel is received, all the nations will glorify God, thus fulfilling the destiny of Israel to be a blessing to the world. This goal, if achieved, will help overcome the conflicts that have so long divided the nations. The restoration of righteousness to the world will occur when nations and races begin to praise God in unity, rather than divisively worshiping and glorifying themselves.

§ § § § § § §

Introduction to These Chapters

There are two excellent places to discover the purpose of Paul's argument in Romans, the introduction in 1:1-15 and the conclusion which begins with 15:14 and continues through 16:27. The technical word for this last portion of Romans is the *peroration*.

In a carefully crafted letter like Romans, the conclusion restates the purpose of writing and appeals for the practical application of the argument. We can see from the content of this peroration that Paul writes to promote his mission. The appeal is for cooperation in the missionary activities in which Paul is involved—in Jerusalem, Rome, and Spain.

Skilled in the art of creating forceful letters, Paul uses the element of emotional appeal recommended by the teachers of the ancient world. We sense the pathos particularly at the end of Chapter 15, and the element of personal involvement in the greetings of Chapter 16.

Here is an outline of this section.

I. Paul's Calling and Strategy (15:14-21)
II. The Appeal to Participate in Mission (15:22-23)
III. The Jerusalem Offering (15:24-29)
IV. First Conclusion to the Letter (15:30-33)
V. The Role of Phoebe (16:1-2)
VI. Greetings to Church Leaders (15:3-16)
VII. The Conclusion of the Book (16:17-27)

Paul's Calling and Strategy (15:14-21)

In this first section, Paul restates his strategy in writing the letter and his own personal calling as a missionary. He describes the connection between the Roman visit and his mission to convert the Gentile world. In wording that is reminiscent of 1:8 and 12, Paul makes clear that he does not consider the Roman church deficient in its expression of the Christian faith. His purpose in writing is not primarily instructive. He explains that he merely provides a *reminder* (verse 15).

While many commentators feel that this statement in verse 15 downplays the significance of his letter too much, the important point to keep in mind is how Paul connects this idea with his own sense of calling to the nations. The purpose of this section is to connect the argument in the main body of Romans with Paul's missionary imperative.

Paul describes his mission as a universal one, aimed at bringing the Gentile nations into obedience to Christ. It is in this context alone that he dares to *be proud of my work for God*. It is clear, however, that he is not bragging about his accomplishments. Rather, he sets his confidence in the calling to be a missionary to the Gentiles. He makes plain in verse 18 that he has no personal achievement in mission. Whatever has been accomplished is because *Christ has wrought through me* the conversion of the Gentiles.

In a striking way Paul describes the means by which God's power has been manifest in the triumph of the gospel. The reference to *word and deed* in verse 18 alludes to the power of the gospel to convert, referring back to the statement of this theme in the thesis of Romans (1:16-17).

Paul goes on to refer to the *signs and wonders* that have attended the preaching of the gospel. This expression refers to the miraculous conversions, healings, and probably also charismatic expressions of faith within early congregations. The *power of the Holy Spirit* has manifested itself in this Gentile mission.

Given the world view of the Roman empire, and of Paul in particular, the gospel is viewed here as moving on the circle of the Mediterranean from Jerusalem around the northern part of the Mediterranean to Iliricum, which is in Yugoslavia, the westernmost point where Paul has preached. His plan now is to come to Rome and have the assistance of its people to move on to Spain (see in 15:24 and 28).

From the way Paul describes his strategy, we can see that he has a sense of urgency to complete the circle. In all probability, the impending sense of the end of the world adds urgency.

Paul's own self-identity in the context of this world mission is that of a *minister of Christ Jesus* to the Gentiles, in ordained service (verse 16). Paul understands himself as the representative of Christ carrying out a priestly and official role in bringing the world into subjection to the Lord by means of the gospel.

The Appeal to Participate in Mission (15:22-23)

In these verses Paul appeals to the congregation to participate with him in his present and future missionary plans.

He opens with the description of his current circumstances. He has now completed his missionary activity in the areas of Corinth, Ephesus, and Macedonia, leaving the responsibility for the expansion of satellite missions in the hands of local leaders. Paul is looking to the west and apparently does not even plan to do any further missionary work in the eastern part of the Roman empire. A confirmation of these plans is found in Acts 20:17-38, where Paul addresses the elders of the Ephesian church and turns leadership responsibilities over to them. He makes it plain that he does not expect to see them again before the end of history.

The Jerusalem Offering (15:24-29)

In verses 24 and 28, we get a clear sense of the kind of cooperation that he hopes to gain from the Roman house churches in staging the Spanish mission. His tact prevents him from asking pointblank for aid, but the expressions that he uses leave no doubt as to what he has in mind.

In verse 24 Paul refers to being *sped on my journey there by you, once I have enjoyed your company for a little*. It sounds very much like the request that comes from relatives for a visit on the way to some distant point. Paul actually implies with this technical expression, *be sped on*, that he wishes to gain missionary support from them. If they support him, he can start his work in the west with their moral support at least, and possibly with some help in the way of people or money.

The same idea is alluded to in 15:28. Here Paul says that after the offering has been delivered to Jerusalem he plans to go on *by way of you to Spain*. Once again, the temporary quality of his plan to visit to Rome is stressed. He hopes to get acquainted in transit, and by implication he hopes to involve the Roman house churches in the planning and support of the Spanish mission.

The peculiar circumstances in Spain made it necessary for Paul to develop a much more substantial support system for his mission there than he had ever had before. The lack of a Jewish population in Spain and the barriers posed by the languages being used there rendered Paul's previous strategy of a self-supporting mission impractical. The entirety of Paul's letter to the Romans is related to developing support for this crucial and very difficult project.

The question of the Spanish mission is closely correlated in this section with the Jerusalem offering. Paul had made an agreement at the time of the apostolic conference in Jerusalem to collect money for the Jerusalem church (Galatians 2:10). He refers here in verse

26 to the two provinces that had been primarily involved in the offering: Macedonia, which would have included the Philippian and Thessalonian churches, and Achaia, which would have included the churches in the area of Corinth.

The rationale for the Jerusalem offering is relevant not only for reconstructing the history of early Christianity, but also for providing a stimulus for stewardship in the modern church.

In verse 27 Paul refers to the fact that the Gentile Christians are in debt to the Jewish Christians. This theme of mutual indebtedness as a motivation for philanthropy was quite characteristic of the ancient world. Gifts were given as a means of communication. They conveyed appreciation for something already received. But gifts were also a means of communication, in that when they were received graciously the person who was in debt was acknowledged as the equal of the person who had originally given the resource. To receive a gift, therefore, meant to acknowledge that someone else was your equal, while to give a gift was to acknowledge that you are subordinate to someone else.

When we place Paul's rationale for the Jerusalem offering in the context of the tensions between conservatives and liberals, Jewish Christians and Gentile Christians, it is clear that he perceives the Jerusalem offering as something of a "peace offering." He apparently hoped that the offering would overcome the tensions between the Jewish Christians and the Gentile Christians. In this sense, the Jerusalem offering is directly connected with the issue of the Spanish mission.

If the Jewish Christian and Gentile Christian tensions continue to divide the Roman churches, the chances of their cooperating in the Spanish mission are nil and the gospel itself is discredited. Therefore, Paul is attempting in these verses to enlist the Roman house churches as his partners in a very delicate political strategy, namely, to unify the competing wings of the early church by means of the Jerusalem offering. If the Roman house churches can be induced to support this project with their prayers, they will have gone a substantial way in the direction of overcoming the tensions within Rome itself, tensions which would jeopardize any possibility of a cooperative mission to Spain. Paul's hope to complete the mission of the known world is directly related to the task of world unification within the church as well as outside the church.

First Conclusion to the Letter (15:30-33)

One of the surprising things about Paul's request for prayer in verses 30-32 is that Paul is not only in danger of being killed by the *unbelievers in Judea*, but also that the Jerusalem offering itself might not be *acceptable to the saints*.

Most scholars agree on the meaning of the first danger. The unbelievers in Judea are clearly the zealous Jews, some of whom may in fact have been related to the Zealot underground movement which was resisting Roman rule at the time Paul was writing this letter. There are references to the plots of such groups against Paul's life in Acts 20:3 and 23:12-35. There is evidence in other Pauline letters of the threat that the Zealot revolutionary movement posed to Paul and other Christian missionaries. It is also likely that the so-called "Judaizer Campaign" to make the Gentile Christians into circumcised Jewish Christians was directly related to Zealot pressures against the Christians in Judea itself.

The Zealot movement in the first century was very much like the modern Ku Klux Klan. It was aimed at preventing racial and religious mixing with Gentiles, and was violently opposed to the continuation of Roman rule over Israel. They used a lynching strategy to enforce conformity with the Jewish law and adherence to the principle of absolute separation between the circumcised and the uncircumcised.

Believing that divine wrath stood against Israel for its disobedience to such absolute principles, they sought to bring about a revolution through violent pressures. It is therefore understandable that Paul would be concerned that he might be *saved*, that is, physically protected from the knives of the assassins. His hope was to deliver the offering and get on to Rome and Spain, not to die as a martyr in Jerusalem.

Given the Zealot threat against Paul's life, it is worth reflecting on how Paul's Jerusalem offering might have appeared to zealous revolutionaries. It appears that they hated Paul with a passion reserved for traitors. Having belonged to the zealous wing of the Pharisees before his conversion, he had become a Christian missionary, a defector to the enemy cause.

A second aspect of Zealot hatred would have related to Paul's successful strategy of approaching the God-fearers among the Gentiles who had been attracted to the Jewish synagogues in the Roman Empire. While Orthodox Jews harbored the hopes that such persons would be converted to full Jewish membership, which involved circumcision and assuming the burden of the Torah, Paul was offering them immediate and unrestricted inclusion in the people of God. Paul was viewed as a kind of rip-off artist, stealing potential Jewish converts with a gospel of cheap grace.

A final provocation was that the Jerusalem offering consisted of Gentile money which Paul insisted on delivering personally in company with prominent Gentiles. For a group believing that even the use of Roman coins was an offense against God, the delivery of such an offering was an outrage.

These considerations help us understand why the offering might not have been *acceptable to the saints*, as Paul feared. The term *saints*, as used in verse 31, probably refers to the conservative Jewish Christians, at this time still under the control of James, the brother of

Jesus. That this conservative group might have been reluctant to receive an offering under these considerations is understandable, in view of the political situation.

If the Jerusalem church had been suffering reprisals from the Zealots, as 1 Thessalonians 2:13-16 reveals, they would surely have been wary about maintaining open relations with the Gentiles. The money that Paul had gathered was clearly Gentile and therefore tainted money, so to receive it publicly entailed the dangers of further Zealot reprisals.

On the basis of these political realities, the significance of Paul's request for intercessory prayer on the part of the Roman house churches becomes clear. In praying to God for the success of the offering, the Roman house churches are praying for the overcoming of the very same tensions which they had experienced internally—tensions between Jewish Christians and Gentile Christians, conservatives and liberals, pro-Romans and anti-Romans.

The benediction of verse 33 concerning *the God of peace* is highly germane to this issue. The task of world unification under the gospel is closely coordinated in Romans with the task of bringing conflicting groups together within the church itself.

The Role of Phoebe (16:1-2)

In light of the peculiar problems posed by the Spanish mission and the disunited churches in Rome, it is significant that Romans ends with so extended a list of greetings to leaders in the Roman house churches, along with a commendation of Phoebe, who is a leader in a church very close to Corinth.

Difficulties in the translation of this passage have led to a misunderstanding of her role in the letter as a whole. A literal translation of these verses is: "I recommend to you Phoebe, our sister who is deacon of the church in Cenchreae, that you receive her with full hospitality in the Lord in a manner suitable of the saints and provide her whatever she needs from you in the matter, for she has also been a patron to many and also to me."

This translation makes it clear that Phoebe is the church leader in Cenchreae, and that she has been a provider of missionary funds and support for a number of early Christian missionaries. She is obviously a person of wealth and a committed church leader. She was planning to travel to Rome, and Paul requests that the Roman house churches *provide her whatever she needs from you in the matter*, which has often puzzled readers. The context, however, makes it plain that *the matter* was the patronage she has provided to other missionaries and now is planning to provide for Paul.

Paul in effect recommends Phoebe as the patroness of the Spanish mission. Her task was to prepare the way for Paul in Rome, to bring and interpret his letter to the Roman house churches, to get them to agree to work together, and to provide the logistical support for Paul's delicate mission to Spain. It was a formidable task whose success was crucial for the Spanish mission.

Greetings to Church Leaders (16:3-16)

Phoebe's activities required the support of the leaders of the Roman house churches, which is why Paul moves immediately from recommending her to greeting all of the church leaders in Rome.

These names fall into several categories. First there is a series of close personal friends and former co-workers in the Pauline mission field who now reside in Rome. We can identify these persons by the fact that Paul makes personal references to his experiences with them. In many instances these would have been the persons who had been banned from Rome under the edict of Claudius in 49. Like Prisca and Aquila, they met Paul in his eastern missionary activities. Since the edict has been lifted now for several years, these persons are now back in Rome.

The fact that, with the exception of Prisca and Aquila, they do not yet appear to be attached to any house churches indicates that these may well be the leaders on whom the tension in Rome has centered. Since Paul knows these leaders personally, he probably can expect their cooperation in the Spanish mission.

Some of the persons greeted are Christians of very long standing. For instance, Andronicus and Junias are a Jewish Christian couple who, according to verse 7, became leaders prior to Paul's own conversion. This means that they had been Christians at least since A.D. 34. Their reputation and activities go back more than twenty years in the rapidly developing early church.

The fact that there are no less than fifteen names in this category gives us a fair indication of the extent of Paul's knowledge of the Roman church situation and his acquaintance with the leaders who had founded several of the small congregations in Rome.

The persons in the second group are known only by hearsay. A recent study of these names has made it clear that those lacking personal references are in all probability ones who had not been in personal contact with him before. If Paul had known all of them personally, the lack of intimate details when compared with things he said about others would have appeared very impolite.

Paul apparently knows the names of these leaders from reports he had received from refugees and travelers. Although Paul does not know these persons individually, the effect of naming them is to honor them. By singling them out, Paul takes the first step in recruiting them, as well as those he knows, for Phoebe's patronage.

In the ancient world naming leaders had an important political function. In the particular situation of the Roman house churches, with the competition between leaders resident in Rome and those returning after the lifting of the edict of Claudius, the naming of competitors in the leadership circle had a politically significant bearing.

The task of political tolerance and inclusion that Paul argues for in 14:1–15:13 is being advanced by the very chapter that many scholars have found quite irrelevant to the presumed doctrinal purpose of Romans.

A Profile of the Roman House Churches

By analyzing the list of names in verses 3-16, a profile of the Roman churches can be developed. Only one of these groups actually calls itself a church. That is the church referred to in 16:3-5, led by Prisca and Aquila. Given their long association with Paul, it is likely that their congregation had an egalitarian approach and essentially a Pauline theology.

It is interesting to observe that the woman's name is almost always mentioned first, contrary to the usual custom in the Greco-Roman world. This indicates that she was either from a higher social class than her husband or was the dominant leader in this particular house church.

The second house church is referred to in verse 10, *those who belong to the family of Aristobulus*. It is clear from this expression that Aristobulus himself is not a Christian, but that there are members of his household who are. The name *Aristobulus* is well known as the grandson of Herod the Great who was a friend of the Emperor Claudius and whose estate was fused into the imperial bureaucracy.

In all probability this group consists of the wealthy slaves and administrators who are handling the former estate of Aristobulus, now part of the imperial properties. In this instance the church had some fairly high connections.

The third church is referred to in verse 11, *those . . . who belong to the family of Narcissus*. The house of Narcissus was one of the major branches of the imperial bureaucracy. It was primarily responsible for imperial correspondence and the conduct of business and legal affairs. The members of this bureaucracy would have been Greek and Roman in their background. And like many other branches of the Roman bureaucracy, they probably had some anti-Semitic tendencies. Once again this is an influential group with very high connections in the Roman government.

The fourth house church is mentioned in verse 14. Here is a series of five leaders whose names are probably those of slaves or freedmen. This group apparently comes from a very different class of people than the first three churches. Paul refers to *the brethren* with them, and there is some likelihood that the group had an egalitarian emphasis. It may have called itself "The Brethren."

The fifth house church is alluded to in verse 15, also with five leaders, three men and two women. Paul refers to the *saints who are with them*, which in the context of early Christian groups probably refers to a more conservative Jewish Christian congregation. A remarkable feature of this church, however, is that, unlike some other Jewish Christian congregations of a conservative bent, they were led by several prominent women.

These five churches each had a very different outlook and different constitution, certainly with different leadership principles and probably different theologies as well. The other resident leaders and itinerant leaders that are mentioned in Chapter 16 with Greek, Roman, and Hebrew names that are recommended as reliable by Paul are probably ones that have not yet been reincorporated into these house churches after the lifting of the edict of Claudius.

The evidence here matches what we discovered in 14:1–15:13. A wide range of theological and ethical distinctions could have caused tensions between these churches because of their very different outlooks.

There would also have been tensions between some of these churches which are now functioning as house churches and the Jewish Christian leaders who are now unattached and apparently unable to find a place in the congregations that they had earlier founded. The task of creating unity in the Roman house churches becomes vividly clear to us when we understand these details.

Many of the leaders mentioned by Paul are women, and some of them are married couples and family members. The close network of friends and relatives that made the early Christian house churches so dynamic and so inclusive is evident here. It was not until the end of the first century that the leadership role of women began to come under serious attack in the Pauline churches. We can see from the very different attitude toward women in the Pastoral Epistles (1 Timothy 2:15; 2 Timothy 3:6-7; Titus 2:3-5), written by the Pauline school toward the end of the first century, how great the change really was. But in the first generation of the Christian mission in the Pauline school it is clear that women played an absolutely essential role.

The Conclusion of the Book (16:17-27)

The conclusion of Romans confirms the missionary purpose of Paul's greatest letter. The aim of Romans was not merely to promote correct theology and ethics, but to urge participation in the world mission. The evidence of church politics points to the proper goal of such activities, not to ensure the ascendency of a particular party within the church, but to sustain the kind of unity within the church that is conducive to world mission.

§ § § § § § §

The Message of Romans 15:14–16:27

Paul seeks unity by respecting the unique potential of each group and each member within the Christian community. There are resources here for the modern church to recover a sense of its mission of world unification, overcoming Zealotism inside and outside the religious communities, and looking for the final triumph of the gospel over the cancer of human sin.

The *obedience of faith* (16:26) is the final goal of the gospel, implying submission to the righteousness of God and hence the restoration of planet earth.

§ § § § § § §

Glossary of Terms

Achaia: A Roman province that included most of the territory of ancient Greece. During Paul's time the proconsul of Achaia was Gallio.

Ampliatus: A man Paul requests the congregation to greet. His identity is unknown.

Andronicus: With Junias, an official Paul requests the congregation to greet (see Romans 16). Could be a distant relative of Paul.

Apelles: A man of unknown identity, designated in Romans 16 as one approved in Christ.

Apostle: A messenger or a person sent for a specific message and mission.

Aquila: The husband of Priscilla (also called Prisca); originally he resided in Corinth but was taken by Paul to Ephesus.

Aristobulus: A Christian mentioned by Paul in Romans 16; his identity is uncertain.

Asyncritus: A Christian man who was greeted by Paul in Romans 16.

Baal: The Canaanite fertility God.

Barbarian: A person incapable of speaking Greek or Latin and thus unable to participate fully in Greco-Roman culture.

Cenchreae: A city on the coast of Greece, near the city of Corinth.

Christ-mysticism: The teaching about the union of

believers in Christ.

Creed: A statement of beliefs often composed for use in Christian worship.

Diatribe: The question-and-answer style of argument; it was designed for the purpose of raising issues with a friendly audience.

Epaenetus: A Christian mentioned by Paul in Romans 16, where he asks the congregation to greet him. His identity is uncertain.

Erastus: Another Christian Paul requests the Romans to greet on his behalf in Romans 16.

Esau: The son of Isaac and Rebekah; the ancestor of the Edomites.

Eschatology: A teaching about the end of the world, which in the case of Romans implies the triumph of God over evil.

Exchange of Lordship: The transfer of believers into the realm where Christ is Lord.

Faith: Loyal response to the gospel of unconditional love in Christ.

Friendly interlocutor: The person, often a student or a friend of the speaker, who poses the questions that are used in a diatribe.

Gaius: A Christian mentioned by Paul in Romans 16, among those Paul requests the congregation to greet. He is also mentioned in the letter to the Corinthians (see 1 Corinthians 1:14).

Gomorrah: A town south of the Dead Sea; punished by God for its wickedness (see Genesis 19).

Grace: The unmerited gift of love, conveyed to humans by the life and death and resurrection of Jesus; an important concept in Pauline theology.

Greco-Roman world: The civilization in the region around the Mediterranean Sea at the time of Paul.

Hermes: A Christian greeted by Paul in Romans 16; his identity is unknown.

Herodion: A Christian greeted by Paul in Romans 16; his

identity is unknown.

House church: The earliest form of Christian community meeting in the home of a church member. The Roman congregations were house churches.

Illyricum: A Roman province located on the eastern coastline of the Adriatic Sea.

Junias: An acquaintance of Paul; possibly a fellow prisoner.

Justification by faith: To be set right by the unconditional love of God, restored to the righteousness intended by God.

Justify: The same as "rightwise;" to make right, and to transform persons in conformity with divine righteousness.

Libertinism: Immoral behavior that was motivated by the belief that one has achieved absolute freedom from the law.

Lucius: A Roman official who was in power during the time of Paul.

Macedonia: The region north of Achaia; it provided the major land route between Asia and the west.

Narcissus: A Christian greeted by Paul in Romans 16.

Natural revelation: The disclosure of God through the natural world, such as seeing divine order in the stars or the seasons.

Nereus: A Christian whose identity is uncertain; he is greeted by Paul in Romans 16.

Olympas: A Christian man who was greeted by Paul in Romans 16.

Patrobas: Also a Christian man Paul greets in Romans 16.

Peroration: The conclusion of an argument, which in the case of Romans is contained in 15:14–16:27.

Persis: A Christian woman whom Paul greets in Romans 16.

Philologus: A Christian man greeted by Paul in Romans 16.

Phlegon: Also greeted by Paul in Romans 16; his exact

identity is uncertain.

Phoebe: A Christian woman who was the deaconness in the church at Cenchreae; Paul recommends her in Romans 16.

Prisca: Wife of Aquila; originally resided in Corinth but was taken by Paul to Ephesus.

Quartus: A Christian man who was greeted by Paul in Romans 16.

Righteousness of God: The capacity and will of the Creator to make the creation conform to divine justice and beauty.

Rabbinic: Pertaining to the Jewish rabbis, or teachers of the law, who were prominent leaders in Paul's time.

Rightwise: To make right, or to achieve a transformation in which humans come to reflect the divine righteousness.

Septuagint: The translation of the Hebrew Scriptures into Greek that was used in the first century.

Sin: The failure to recognize human limitations, which in Romans is marked by suppressing the truth.

Sodom: A city located south of the Dead Sea; it was punished by God for its great wickedness (see Genesis 19).

Sosipater: A Christian man greeted by Paul in Romans 16.

Stachys: A Christian man also greeted by Paul in Romans 16.

Tertius: A Christian man to whom Paul dictated the letter to the Romans (see Romans 16:22).

Tryphaena: With Tryphosa, Christian women who were greeted by Paul in Romans 16.

Tryphosa: See above.

Universal sin: The doctrine that each person fails to accept and live out the truth about God and human obligations.

Urbanus: A Christian man who was greeted by Paul in Romans 16.

Wrath: The punishment of those who violate divine righteousness, which in Romans is experienced in everyday life.

Zealotism: Fanatical adherence to the perceived will of God, which confuses the distinction between divine and human values.

Guide to Pronunciation

Achaia: Ah-KAY-ah
Andronicus: An-DROH-nih-kus
Aquila: Ah-KWIH-lah
Ampliatus: Am-plee-AH-tus
Apelles: Ah-PELL-us
Aristobulus: Air-iss-TAH-bih-lus
Asyncritus: Ah-SIN-crih-tus
Baal: Bah-AHL
Cenchreae: SEN-kree-ah
Epaenetus: Ee-PAY-neh-tus
Erastus: Eh-RAS-tus
Esau: EE-saw
Gaius: GAY-us
Gomorrah: Guh-MORE-ah
Hermas: HER-mas
Hermes: HER-mees
Herodion: Heh-ROH-dee-on
Illyricum: Ih-LEER-ee-cum
Junias: JOO-nee-as
Lucius: LOO-shus
Macedonia: Ma-seh-DOH-nee-ah
Narcissus: Nar-SIH-sus
Nereus: NEE-ree-us
Olympas: Oh-LIM-pas
Patrobas: PAT-roh-bas
Persis: PER-sis

Philologus: Fih-loh-LOH-gus
Phlegon: FLEH-gon
Phoebe: FEE-bee
Prisca: PRIH-sah
Quartus: KWAR-tus
Sodom: SOD-um
Sosipater: Sah-SIP-ah-ter
Stachys: STAY-kis
Tertius: TER-tee-us
Tryphaena: Treh-FAY-nah
Tryphosa: Treh-FOH-sah
Urbanus: Ur-BAN-us

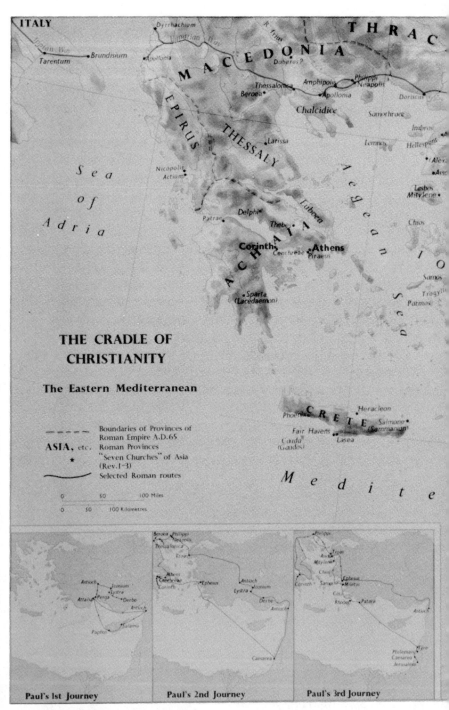

THE CRADLE OF
CHRISTIANITY

The Eastern Mediterranean

- - - - - Boundaries of Provinces of
Roman Empire A.D.65
ASIA, etc. Roman Provinces
★ "Seven Churches" of Asia
(Rev.1-3)
Selected Roman routes

0   50   100 Miles

0   50   100 Kilometres

Paul's 1st Journey

Paul's 2nd Journey

Paul's 3rd Journey

ASIA MINOR

From the *Oxford Bible Atlas*, Third Edition

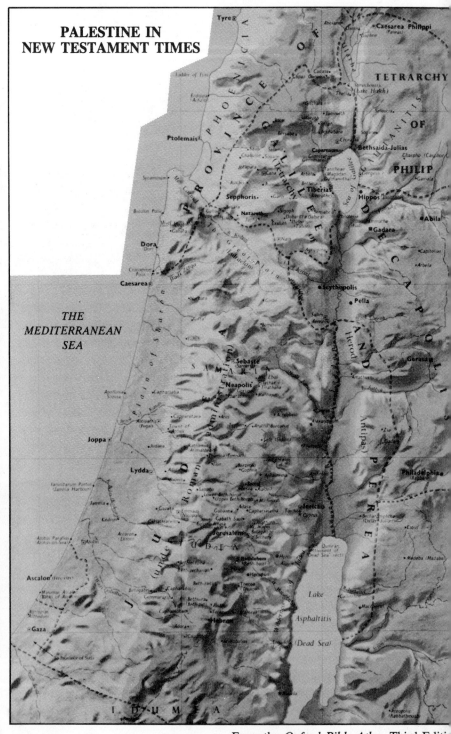

PALESTINE IN
NEW TESTAMENT TIMES

THE
MEDITERRANEAN
SEA

From the *Oxford Bible Atlas*, Third Editio